THE
INTERVIEW

A Pangaro Training Guide
Essential for Police, Corrections and All Law Enforcement

Lt. Joseph J. Pangaro

Looseleaf Law Publications, Inc.

43-08 162nd Street
Flushing, NY 11358
www.LooseleafLaw.com
800-647-5547

Library of Congress Cataloging-in-Publication Data

Names: Pangaro, Joseph J., 1962- author.
Title: The interview : a Pangaro training guide essential for police, corrections and all law enforcement / Lt. Joseph J. Pangaro (Ret.), CPM, CSO, MOI.
Description: New York : Looseleaf Law Publications, Inc., [2021] | Includes index. | Summary: "The Role of the Police Officer, Detective and Correctional Officer, Action Imperatives, Active Listening Skills, Understanding the Difference Between Interview and Interrogation, Understanding Human Nature, Pre-Interview Conversation, The Four Techniques for Successful Interviewing, Interview Preparation, Understanding Human Nature, Understanding Interrogation, Kids vs. Adult interviews, False Confessions"-- Provided by publisher.
Identifiers: LCCN 2020036958 (print) | LCCN 2020036959 (ebook) | ISBN 9781608852260 (paperback) | ISBN 9781608852277 (ebook)
Subjects: LCSH: Interviewing in law enforcement. | Police questioning. | Criminal investigation.
Classification: LCC HV8073.3 .P36 2021 (print) | LCC HV8073.3 (ebook) | DDC 363.25/4--dc23
LC record available at https://lccn.loc.gov/2020036958
LC ebook record available at https://lccn.loc.gov/2020036959

Cover by: *Alfredo Rico* - www.ricovisuals.com

Table of Contents

Acknowledgments i

Dedication ii

About the Author iii

Introduction xv

Chapter 1 - The Art of Interview 1
   THE BASICS 1
   THE IMPORTANT ROLES OF THE PATROL OFFICER,
      DETECTIVE OR CORRECTIONS OFFICER 2
   WHO CAN ASK QUESTIONS? 3
   THE VALUE OF INTROSPECTION 4

Chapter 2 – Important Concepts for Conducting Good
   Interviews 7
   COGNITIVE DISSONANCE 7
   JEOPARDY 12
   POSSIBILITIES 14
   ACTION IMPERATIVES 17
   WHAT ARE ACTIVE LISTENING SKILLS? 18
   MORE ABOUT POSSIBILITIES 20
   PRE-INTERVIEW CONVERSATION AND SETTING A
      BASELINE FOR RESPONSES. 20
   WORDS MEAN THINGS. LANGUAGE HAS POWER. 23
   THE POWER OF HUMAN COMPASSION AND HUMAN TOUCH ... 24
   PUSH LINES—MOVING CONVERSATION TO CONFESSION 27

Chapter 3 – The Interview Starts Off 31
   PROPER GREETINGS 31
   PROMISES 35
   RESPECT 36
   WHAT IS A SOCIOPATH? 38

Chapter 4 – The Art of Interview—Why Do I Call it an Art?. 39
   DEFINITION 39
   BONDING 40
   WHAT IS COVERED 40

UNDERSTANDING THE DIFFERENCE BETWEEN AN
    INTERVIEW AND AN INTERROGATION AND WHEN
    EACH SHOULD BE USED 41
UNDERSTANDING HUMAN NATURE 41

Chapter 5 – Who Makes a Good Interviewer? 45
PEOPLE WHO INTERVIEW 45
CURIOSITY 46
DOING THE WORK 50
WORDS MEAN THINGS 51
A LIFE LESSON- "JOE AND CHUCK ON THE STREET"............ 51
A QUICK QUESTION: DOES DECEPTION MEAN GUILT? 55

Chapter 6 – The Miranda Warnings 57
FIRST IMPRESSIONS 57
POLICE CUSTODY 57
HERE'S MY THEORY ON MIRANDA WAIVER 58

Chapter 7–Interacting with Suspects,
Victims and Witnesses 61
REALITY AND PROFESSIONALISM..................................... 61
PRE-INTERVIEW CONVERSATIONS 61
LIGHTS, CAMERA, ACTION – IT'S YOUR SHOW –
    VIDEO/DIGITAL RECORDING OF INTERVIEWS 64

Chapter 8 – The Four Main Techniques, The Keys
to the Kingdom 69
DIMINISHING.. 69
RATIONALIZING 72
OFFER ALTERNATIVES 76
DISPLAYING COMPASSION.. 77
BUILDING A BOND 78

Chapter 9 – Human Reactions 81
PHYSICAL SIGNALS TO LOOK FOR DURING AN INTERVIEW..... 81
A CASE STUDY / SEX OFFENDER INTERVIEW 82

Chapter 10 – Interview Preparation 89
PERSONAL INVENTORY... 89
THE UNDERSTANDING AND USE OF POSSIBILITIES 89
WHY DO THEY LIE?.. 91
SO WHERE DO WE GET THE POSSIBILITIES? 91

HERE'S HOW IT WORKS—DIMINISHING THE
    DESCRIPTION OF THE CRIME 92
RATIONALIZING ACTIONS 93
THE INVESTIGATOR MUST UNDERSTAND HUMAN NATURE ... 95
FIRST OBSTACLE 95
WHY? 96
THE STAGES OF AN INTERVIEW 97
UNDERSTANDING INTERROGATION 98
"PUSH LINES" 100
OTHER THINGS TO LOOK FOR 101
STRESS AND BODY LANGUAGE 102
MICRO GESTURES 105
OTHER BODY LANGUAGE THINGS TO BE AWARE OF 105

Chapter 11 – Case Study: Two Kinds of Guys 109
    TWO KINDS OF GUYS 109

Chapter 12 – Other Considerations 115
    CULTURAL DIFFERENCES IN INTERVIEWS 115
ADULTS VS. CHILDREN 118
NORMAL VS. SOCIOPATH 120
OLDER SUSPECTS 120
MENTALLY CHALLENGED PEOPLE 121
FALSE CONFESSIONS 123
INTERVIEWING SOMEONE AFTER A VIOLENT ARREST 127
THE END OF THE BEGINNING 128

Conclusion 131

Index 133

Acknowledgments

There are a number of people I want to thank for helping make this book possible. No one gets anywhere in life alone; we all have many people who have helped shape us, mentor us, love us, educate us, comfort us, criticize us, and inspire us. We are the sum of all this effort, and I am no different.

Let's start with my wife Kathleen, who has supported me throughout my career. She has been there for the triumphs and the trials as I went from private citizen to sworn police officer and then moved between the ranks and divisions of my police agency. From the patrol division and the shift work, missed holidays, forced overtime, nights and weekend work, to the detective bureau and the endless call-ins, phone calls and court dates, to supervision and the soul searching to be the best leader I could be, Kathleen was there every minute, always encouraging me. I could not have had the career I had without her.

Next up are my kids: Joseph, Alexander, Marisa Joy and Jack, as well as my daughters-in-law, Addie and Melissa, all of whom have made my life better and showed me what love really means.

To my police and prosecution partners, Lance Rowland, Bill Koch, Chuck Weinkofsky, Jeff Layton, Kevin McDermott, Mike Pembleton, Ken Kennedy, Phil Miller, Matt Sharin, Annie Samuels, Elaine Leschot, Thomas Campo, and Gary D'Esposito, in particular. These men and women took me under their wings and helped me to understand my role as a police officer and how to do the job well.

To my favorite professor, Bub Kovacs, who had more influence on my thinking then he will ever know.

To Mary Loughrey, my publisher, who read my initial submission and saw something she believed was valuable and gave me a chance to offer this material to you in the hope that I can help you be the best investigator you could be.

And, finally, to all of people who have taken a few minutes out of their busy lives to read any of my articles or honored me by attending my classes. None of this would be possible without all these people and I love you all.

Dedication

This book is dedicated to two groups of people that I love. First, my wife Kathleen and my children: Joseph, Alex, Marisa and Jack and my daughters-in-laws, Addie and Melissa. They all lived the life of a police family with me: the ups and downs, the irregular shifts and missed holidays, the late night and weekend callouts, and the feelings of never being sure I would come home.

It was their support for me and my chosen profession that allowed me to give 100% of my energy to the task at hand—protecting and serving my community.

I also want to dedicate this book's concepts, wisdom and stories to all of my brothers and sisters in law enforcement and corrections: those who came before me, those on the job now, those who have retired after serving their communities and those will come after us, the next wave of the Blue Line. Our country cannot survive without a steady flow of men and women willing to don the uniform, strap on the gun and walk the dangerous streets of our towns, cities, jails, and prisons, following a calling bigger than their own needs.

I hope this book helps you do the work you swore an oath to do and your community needs you to do.

—Lt. Joseph Pangaro

About the Author

One of the first things I tell anyone who is trying to learn anything is to ask: *"Who are the people giving you the information? What is their background? Do they have any real experience or expertise in the area they are presenting or are they simply regurgitating what someone else told them?"*

In other words, experience in real world activities is the best source of knowledge.

The world of law enforcement, like other professional arenas, has some great practitioners. They have put in their time to learn the concepts and ideas about the profession and then, most important, they have actually applied these lessons to real-life situations. Unfortunately, there are also quite a few people who talk a good game but can't really perform in the real world, let alone be successful, which is why I have included this section in my book.

I want you to know my background and who I am so you will know that I am not simply telling you what I conjecture might work, but because my opinions are based on my real-life experiences.

I started my career in 1986 in a municipal police agency in central New Jersey on the Shore. The community was a mix of social, economic and racial demographics. Forty-seven different languages were spoken in our middle schools. We had million-dollar homes, thousands of apartment units, lower-end housing and highway motels that rented by the hour, day, week, or month.

The people who lived in the community included some of the wealthiest people in the state as well as many people who were struggling to make a living day to day and, unfortunately, many people who survived on public assistance and other forms of supplemental income.

We had a huge shopping / retail environment that included a state-of-the-art shopping mall, movie theaters, banks, strip malls, restaurants and other outlets where people gathered daily to spend their money.

Our population at bedtime was about 35,000 residents, but it swelled to over 125,000 during the day. Three major highways crossed the borders and ran through town as well as numerous county roads and a NJ Transit Rail line.

The towns that surrounded our community included Asbury Park and Long Branch, two icons of the Jersey Shore, as well as Tinton Falls, Neptune Township, Deal, Interlaken, and Eatontown. This group of communities reflected every social and economic division of the entire country, from the very rich to the very poor and everything in between. It was a challenging place to be a police officer.

We used to say you could be as busy as you wanted to be on any given shift outside of your calls for service. If you were having a bad day and were a bit tired you could take it easy in some of the residential areas or if you were looking for a more involved night you could stop and arrest someone with a gun or drugs on almost any corner.

In addition to the heavy vehicle traffic that came through town at all hours of the day and night, there was an active presence of people on foot, especially along the highways and in the shopping areas. It was an opportune place to use, practice and hone your investigative skills on any given day or shift.

When I joined the force in 1986, I was new to the ideas and concepts of police work, and coming onto the job was exciting and a bit unnerving. I had no real experience with police work other than the stories I heard from a cousin who was a cop, Charlie Ackerman. My hometown was a low-crime area where the most noteworthy crimes were soaping windows and bashing mailboxes, which did not prepare me for what was to come during my career.

I was in for a great surprise when I began working the streets. I was exposed to people from every race and nationality you could imagine. I went to houses where the people made more money in a week than I would my entire career. And I went to homes where the parents were drunk or high and beat and sometimes killed their kids. There were places where girls and women, including elderly women, were raped by nighttime burglars.

It was quite a learning experience. I realized very quickly that my naive understanding of people and how they lived and acted was very different from my own life. I watched some really great ROAD COPS handle crazy calls and even crazier people. I saw how they talked to them, fought with them and dealt with the terrible things they saw during a shift.

I was blessed that many of these great cops took me under their wing and showed me the ropes. They told me when I was doing something correctly and, more importantly, when I was doing something stupid. They looked out for me, mentored me and showed me how to tell when someone was lying or trying to get one over, or using my own inexperience against me.

It didn't take long for me to learn these lessons, and I began to develop my own style. I was aggressive and I loved the immediacy of patrol work: stopping cars, responding to robbery calls, meeting people on the street and other in-your-face types of calls.

I could feel my confidence growing day by day and the results of what I was doing could be seen in the quality and quantity of the arrests I was making. I went from arrests for dime bags of pot possessed by teenagers to much larger seizures held by experienced drug dealers.

My roadside interviews improved to the point that I managed to get confessions from burglars, thieves and other street criminals on a regular basis, and I loved it.

However, it soon became clear to me that there was one underlying skill that I had to enhance, which was the ability to talk to people. At the time, however, I didn't call it that; I called it being good at B.S.

What I thought was just talking to someone was really what I found to be the key to successful police work, the ability to connect with another person, no matter who they were or where they came from or how much money that had, and have a conversation with them.

This realization was the turning point in my police career. Suddenly, it didn't matter that I came from a small town with no crime to speak of. If I could find a way to connect with the person I was talking to, I could get them to tell me things like who did it, why they did it and where the evidence was, I would be successful.

I also realized that anyone could do this, but many cops don't see the ramifications of making these connections.

As my performance improved, my stats went up and I made better arrests and developed informants all over the place. As the detectives began to make good cases off my informants, they took notice of me and began to include me in some of their work, such as surveillance jobs, stakeouts and drug raids.

After nine years on the road an opening in the detective bureau became available and I got the position.

Joining the detective bureau was one of the most exciting times of my career. Although I loved the patrol division and the work we did, the detective bureau was an absolute thrill and an undeniable change of pace.

I was now wearing a suit, coming and going as I needed to and, best of all, I was dealing with the worst of the worst in criminals—real criminals. Another aspect of the work that I found both exciting and concerning was that the buck stopped at my desk.

As a patrol officer, I investigated a crime, took a report and passed it off to the detectives, there was no responsibility of tracking down the suspects or getting a confession. But as a detective the case folder for the robbery, the rape or the stabbing ended up on my desk; and with the folder came the responsibility of solving the crime and getting some justice for the victims.

This part of the new job was one that weighed heavily on me. I wanted to do a good job and I wanted to be confident that I could handle whatever came my way. It was here that I was blessed a second time by getting to work with some great old-school detectives that were excellent at their craft.

I watched my fellow detectives conduct interviews with some very bad players—individuals who murdered, raped, robbed and hurt people very badly. These detectives were amazing. They were very cool, calm and collected.

They would go into an interview with a suspect and chat with them for half an hour before moving onto the criminal aspects of the case; and even then, it didn't look like it did on TV.

They got more aggressive for sure, but they never hit anyone or smacked anyone with a phone book à la Andy Sipowicz on the *NYPD Blue* TV show. Instead, they "talked" with them, calmed them and reasoned with them. They were relentless and seemingly tireless in their interviews, some that lasted hours.

I still remember the feeling of utter astonishment when the first serial rapist case I was on ended with the suspect admitting to the detective what he had done and why. In fact, the suspect was crying during his confession statement and seemed concerned that the detective thought badly of him for his crimes.

I knew at that moment I wanted to achieve that skill level of interviewing. I was sent to many different kinds of training for forensics, statement taking, crime scene investigation and other essential detective-related courses. Without a doubt, the most important aptitude to be developed as an effective interviewer was the ability to interact with a person and establish a bond with them.

Teaching this aspect of police work was difficult. Many trainers could teach you how to do a physical task like lifting latent fingerprints or packing evidence, but they had real problems finding a way to teach you the subtleties how to connect with another person.

It was then that my partner and I began to talk about this skill in depth. We talked about what worked and why and how each of us found ways to make the connection, even with some very bad people.

Clearly, connecting with a person and building a bond in terms of law enforcement work does not mean being their buddy or even liking them. What it does entail is finding that one tactic or personal trait you have to connect with the person you are investigating and make them feel comfortable enough to talk to you.

Over time we called these skills our *schtick*, which is a term used by old vaudeville performers; it was their routine, their act. We understood that much of what we were doing was a practiced skill or set routine that we could use when dealing with suspects, victims and witnesses. As time went on, we honed these skills, perfected them as best as we could and used them all the time.

Our confession rate was impressive. It got to the point that many of the cops at headquarters would joke that they never wanted to have to sit across a table from us if they did anything wrong. This was the most significant compliment we could have ever received—respect and recognition from other cops.

It was then that I realized what was missing in most police courses was addressing the humanization factor. Police work is always presented as a hard-nosed, fact-based activity. However, it became apparent to me that there was much more to it than that. In fact, investigating was really an art form all on its own and that's when I started making notes about the process. I created a course and taught it to other police officers. I found I could relate the skills in clear language, using real techniques learned on the job to make the examples readily accessible to fellow cops. I found that I could help a lot of officers by putting these techniques, stories and concepts into a book format. This is how the *Art of Interview* was conceived.

I served as a detective for the next 11 years and I could not have been happier. During my tenure, we concentrated on all types of active crimes, including serial rapists, serial burglars, economic crime, vice crimes, gambling, homicide, sex crimes and lots of drug work.

Every day was an adventure and I couldn't wait to get to work. You never knew what you would be walking into. On many days I would come in and one of my partners in the detective bureau would be feverishly typing away on a search warrant— "Go dress down we're doing a paper at 6 PM," they would yell, and it was game on.

"Doing a paper" meant serving a search warrant; and there was nothing better than serving a search warrant! We used to laugh and describe the process as: "A judge just gave us an ORDER to go kick down a door and search some criminal's house." It was thrilling.

Over time, we used the search warrant as an indispensable tool of our trade to gather evidence that would pass court muster. Over the course of one to two years we were running 80 to 100 warrants a year from our 10-man detective bureau. For perspective, the average number of yearly warrants executed by the county's narcotics strike force were 75 to 80 search warrants during the same time period, but they covered the entire county. Indeed, whenever the boss would assign case files, the first thing we would do was read over them to "Find the search warrant in the case." We became experts in writing and serving search warrants on every type of crime from drugs to murders, assaults, vice, and economic crimes.

My interview skills grew during these years and I became very confident in using them, although I never lost that feeling of amazement about a serious criminal's confession. I would sit there and shake my head realizing the power of these skills and that anyone could learn them if they had a mind to do it. After all I had.

I think it's important to keep in mind that anyone can learn these techniques to be an effective interviewer. It takes a desire to excel at it, a willingness to learn and practice the skills. If you do that you too will become a good interviewer.

In 2005 I was promoted to the rank of Sergeant and maintained my assignment to the detective bureau, which was another proud moment. In our department there was an unwritten rule that if you got promoted you had to serve as a supervisor in the patrol division or you would not really get experience as a supervisor.

I never understood that assumption, but it went something like this: "If you want to learn to supervise you have to monitor 8 to 10 officers out on the road as they answer calls for service and conduct police work."

I always thought that the ROAD COPS knew how to do their jobs very well. They backed each other up, they knew when to take their breaks and they served the township properly.

On the other hand, I believed supervising detectives was more of a challenge because they conducted much of their work outside of the township, in other jurisdictions, serving search warrants and acting in plainclothes under the radar. This was a challenge when you had active, aggressive officers that were always on the move.

Either way, I was assigned to a position in the bureau where I got to lead the officers and help choose new recruits. This was a salient part of my career and one I took very seriously. I hated the old system of picking most detectives because of who they knew or were friends with or who's kid was the chief's son's pal. I always believed that the best, hardest-working cops should get the valued positions, like detective, based on merit.

I was well-suited for this role, and it taught me a lot about supervision; that is, how to do it right and what characteristics indicated a poor leader. I tried to actually live the things I believed in such as Servant Leadership, which meant the higher rank you attained in an organization the more you owed to those below you. Leadership positions should not be self-aggrandizing opportunities, but rather opportunities to serve your subordinates and your organization, share your experience and help everyone get better at what they do. Sounds corny, I know, but I believe it and I live it to this day.

In 2006, I applied for a lieutenant's position that had opened, and I was promoted for the second time in 18 months; this time, I was transferred to the patrol bureau.

Because of my belief in serving my men and women, I found myself locking horns with the chief. And we all know how that goes; I was promoted and moved to patrol. Back to weekends and nights, but at a much higher pay rate. I took it as an opportunity to pass on my experience to the next generation and lead from where I was.

As part of my new position I was tasked with running the training bureau. Although some believed the chief did this to punish me, I saw it as another blessing. Detective work was my first love but teaching was quickly gaining ground as another favorite interest. It was a way of giving back to the cops that had mentored me, closing the circle if you would.

In addition to revamping the training bureau and bringing us into the future as far as training opportunities and activities were concerned, I was also determined to enhance the thinking about police work and move the agency to the forefront of how to conduct police work in general and investigations in particular.

Based on the success I had in this mission, I looked optimistically toward the future. Retirement from police work was not far off, and I wanted to find a way to stay connected to the profession and continue to make a difference.

In 2009, I started my own company to provide training courses based on actual, in-the-field experiences to the officers in my state and region. Since the company's inception, we have created a huge footprint in the police training world and we are expanding each year.

Another one of my responsibilities as a lieutenant was to perform Internal Affairs (IA) investigations. Although this is not something any cop wants to do, it is a necessary function of police work.

The classic view of IA cops is that they are out to get people, ruin their careers for nothing and act as a hammer for a police administration to attack PBA/ FOP or other union reps and cops that don't toe the administration's line. I hated that.

Me and a friend, a Captain in the Patrol Bureau, decided to change the paradigm on IA work. We made it more user-friendly and conducted fact-based investigations without any political or personality overtones.

Some of our most-effective cases involved cops that we didn't particularly like as people. We treated them fairly no matter how much the temptation was to look extra negatively at their actions. In fact, we made sure if and when we cleared them, we did so loudly! It was the only appropriate thing to do—it was fair and it served the agency. I always believed that in an IA case, if an officer or officers were proved to be innocent of the charges against them, the IA bureau should scream it from the rooftops. It was only fair.

As the year 2013 rolled around I began to see my future path more clearly. I had served for 27 years and my training company was growing. I found satisfaction in the training and being a businessman. Several years earlier I was given an opportunity to write for a local newspaper about what it's like to be cop. That column has been running weekly since 2010, which led to a monthly column in *BLUE* magazine and several articles in the *FBI* magazine and other police publications in other countries.

With so many irons in the fire, I decided to take my retirement. In June 2013 I left the building for the last time as a full-time officer and began my new life as a teacher and trainer, and I haven't looked back for a minute.

Although I do miss the energy of police work, I love the opportunity to help make my profession better and be a part of the lives of the officers still serving through my writing, teaching and training. One of the older guys that retired several years before me put it very well—"I miss the clowns but not the circus!"

Teaching, training and writing keeps me connected to the profession I love. This book is another example on my part to give back. I hope the ideas in this book help you be a great cop and do good work during your career. Ours is a noble profession, worthy of our sacrifice and our best efforts. Always keep learning, seeking the truth and moving forward, and never miss an opportunity to help another cop on their journey.

So, in part, that's who I am. I wanted you to know; not because I am looking for accolades or to impress you, but so you can be confident in the things you read here. All the lessons and stories are gleaned from real life, real cases and real encounters with people for the purpose of revealing many of the concepts, ideas and tactics that have worked successfully in the real world, so you can use them in your town or city, with the people you must serve as a police officer.

I am honored that you would buy this book and read it. I know the information on these pages will help you on your career journey. Make notes in the margins, dog-ear the pages, use a highlighter and make the most of the information. From one cop to another—be safe and do a great job!

Sincerely,

Lt. Joseph Pangaro *(Ret.)* CPM, CSO, MOI

Introduction

In the modern world of law enforcement and criminal investigation it is crucial that the officer conducting criminal investigations have a solid understanding of several critical skill areas including highly technical information, interpersonal skills, and the use of available technology. Without these critical areas of knowledge, the officer will not be successful.

Of these areas of knowledge, the interpersonal skill set is the most important, because police work, at its essence, is a person-to-person business. This aspect of law enforcement work is often overlooked, because many believe that facts are the only important part of an investigation.

Although facts alone can provide insight into an incident, it is only through human interaction that we will get the total picture of an incident; therefore, police work is a very personal and intimate interaction between people. If you fail to see it that way you will miss out on a tremendous advantage that we can use to solve crime, build relationships and become an accomplished investigator.

This is a truth that I learned through many years of actual experience out in the field. It is the linchpin of successful law enforcement. Therefore, with each area we cover in this book I will present the "Human Connection" aspect of the learning.

Diversity in the Ranks

Before we go any further, I must address two things. First, when I discuss how to conduct interviews or take any other action and I describe suspects, victims or witnesses I often use male gender terms such as "he" or "him." An example "When you talk to the suspect you want get him to ..." or "The investigator wants to get himself in the right mindset...."

This does not mean that I'm overlooking the use of "she" or "her"; in fact, I do try to write it to include both male and female terms such as: "When you ask the suspect what he/she had for dinner," I just don't always indicate it that way. So, let's be clear—when I say "he" for the cop or the suspect, "she" is also implied.

Second, it must be acknowledged that the role of women in law enforcement has grown steadily over the years. Women now occupy a variety of positions in many agencies, including road cops, detectives, supervisors, executives and chiefs. This is a good thing for women and our society.

I have always been a proponent of women in law enforcement. I have worked with some of the best cops and prosecutors in the business and many of them have been women. The women I've worked with have taught me and mentored me and I am very appreciative of all their efforts. Some were hard-as-nails street cops, others were compassionate supervisors that led the men and women of their agency with strength and courage and a perspective that was needed in law enforcement.

That is one of the most valuable things I have seen happen to law enforcement over the years, the inclusion of women among the ranks. Women bring a different perspective to every area of police work, which benefits all of our communities, cities and towns.

So, if I say "he," please read it as he or she, OK? We are all in this together.

Chapter 1 - The Art of Interview

THE BASICS

We start our dive into this interviewing process by understanding some basics, like *"Who should read this book?"* and *"Who can learn these concepts?"*

The answers here are the same for both questions.... "Any police officer, detective, investigator, corrections officer or supervisor needs to know how to conduct interviews properly and professionally, they are the lifeblood of police work and will solve more cases and change more lives than almost any evidence." And while this book is for police and corrections officers and investigators, in reality, anyone who has to conduct interviews should give it a read to enhance their skills.

I have had many young officers say to me "I'm only a patrol officer or a deputy or a corrections officer." When they say it there is almost a resignation that they are nothing more than report takers, which is wrong. A patrol officer or deputy or corrections officer are the first line of the law enforcement family and the people that usually initially come into contact with the citizens of our communities first.

These positions, though usually where most officers start their careers, are vital to the safety of your community. The patrol officer, deputy and corrections officers are the backbone of any law enforcement agency; they are key to the success of the law enforcement mission.

Besides that, I know many great cops that are dedicated to the uniformed law enforcement career and would never consider leaving the road, and I say bravo to them.

The message I want you to take away is simple though, EVERY person in the law enforcement profession, no matter if you wear a suit or a uniform, walk a beat, push a radio car or patrol the most dangerous precincts in our nation—the jails and prisons of our country—must develop their interview skills, it is something you do every day.

THE IMPORTANT ROLES OF THE PATROL OFFICER, DETECTIVE OR CORRECTIONS OFFICER

The patrol officer and the detective must realize the importance of his/her role in the criminal investigations procedure as well as the eventual prosecution of criminal acts in the judicial system. Although there is a belief in many departments that the patrol officer simply responds to calls for service and takes reports, I do not subscribe to that theory at all.

Every officer is also a criminal investigator. Although his/her duties do not always allow for the ongoing investigation or follow-up of all criminal incidents, he/she handles in their initial stages, the officer must view themselves as a criminal investigator and act accordingly.

Historically, it has not been the policy of many Police Departments that the patrol officer should fully investigate each and every incident they are assigned or initiate on their own, but I believe the patrol officer should make a concerted effort to uncover as many facts about an incident as possible. Therefore, the officer should seek to identify any and all witnesses, evidence and perpetrators involved in any case they are assigned.

The aim of this book is to provide guidance and instruction to the patrol officer and the detective in the best practices to use on a consistent basis while investigating any type of incident and to enhance the interview skills of everyone tasked with investigating criminal activity.

A specific skill set addressed in this book is that of interviewing suspects, witnesses and victims. I refer to this as the Art of Interview, and to do it correctly you must understand the concepts of how people respond and interact with other people. It is not a one-size-fits-all process, but rather an ever-evolving flow, a give and take of information between those involved. Doing it right is an art form and you can learn to be a great artist.

Just as every great artist is unique in how they create their art, so to the great interviewer is unique because of her/ his personality, life experiences, natural talents and learned skills. When we use these individual qualities together with what we learn and practice, we all can grow and be better.

> *"This is it; this is what separates good cops from great investigators—Interview skills."*
>
> —Lt. J. Pangaro

Let's get started...

WHO CAN ASK QUESTIONS?

—*"Did you do it?"*

A tenacious investigator takes an answer of "No, I didn't" and turns it into a confession that sends a bad person to prison and away from the rest of decent society for as long as possible.

Like any skill, the ability to be a great interviewer demands we understand not only how the techniques work but why. The why means understanding how human beings interact and talk to each other. This concept of communication between people is at the heart of interviewing and is something I reference all the time.

Ask yourself some questions—

> *"Am I a people person?"*
>
> *"Am I good at small talk?"*
>
> *"How do I come across to people?"*
>
> *"Do I rub people the wrong way?"*
>
> *"Do I make people feel comfortable?"*
>
> *"Do I have the gift of gab?"*
>
> *"Am I a blowhard or a bully?"*
>
> *"Am I confident in my skills?"*

Your answers—honest answers—to these simple questions about yourself can help you develop as an interviewer. This self-introspection is very important to growth, especially if you have to interact with other people to be successful.

THE VALUE OF INTROSPECTION

As human beings we have to understand our strengths and weaknesses. If we don't or if we ignore specific aspects of our personality that we don't like, then we are not going to achieve our best result in any endeavor we undertake. It is imperative that you look deep into yourself to understand who your really are. That is why I believe that self-introspection is so important for anyone to get better at anything. If we don't enhance our strengths and mitigate our weaknesses, we cannot grow as a person or as an interviewer.

Your answers can become a guide as to what you need to work on to be a better communicator and interviewer. We all know people who are easy or terrible to talk to. A good interviewer uses Active Listening skills, a proper demeanor, tact, intellect, and street smarts to get the answers they need. We all have room for change, understanding what we need to change is often the problem.

> *Important concept here:*
> *Every interaction between people is an interview.*

An interview is a question and answer period; a time to exchange information with a suspect, witness or unwitting. (*Unwitting* is a term used to describe a person who doesn't know they are helping the police or doesn't know they are involved in an investigation. The dictionary defines unwitting as: A person not aware of the full facts.) This is a place where you ask a question and the suspect answers it or the suspect asks you a question about your question. It's a give and take of information with a goal in mind.

You should not overlook the importance of this concept. People will only communicate honestly with someone they have developed a trust for, even if it is only a fleeting trust. The back and forth of any conversation allows us to explore many aspects of the relationship that is developing.

Consider meeting someone you want to have a personal relationship with, especially a romantic relationship. The initial conversations are filled with "testing" questions as you both try to understand—who is the person I am with? Do I like them? To some degree we all consider things like- Is the person safe, are they smart, are they funny, do I get a good feeling from them. All of these basic judgements take place lightning fast in the background and the thing that propels the encounter forward are the internal responses we feel as we talk. If the relationship here is going to go forward both people have to feel OK with it. Same in an interview.

The goal of this part of the interview, the beginning, is for you to size up the person being interviewed. What are they all about? What makes them tick, what motivates them, what concerns them?

As you talk to the person you will want to see if you can identify a subject's interest in the conversation and what information they may be willing to share or hide from you. Using a fishing term, you use your questions as bait to lure them in and if they show interest and engage you by taking the bait, you let the suspect run out with some line, like a fish on a reel. A question is a piece of bait. You throw it out in the interview to see what the suspect sniffs at, what gets his/her attention. If he/she bites on a topic and takes the bait, you let them run.

Chapter 2 - Important Concepts for Conducting Good Interviews

Before we go any further, I think this is a good time to consider and get comfortable with some important concepts relating to how people interact with each other. Understanding them here will help as we move through the rest of the material in the book and the examples I will give to illuminate my points.

Some of the important concepts include:

- **Cognitive Dissonance** – what that means and how it can be used to help you identify deception.

- **Jeopardy** and how it affects human interactions and responses

- **Possibilities** – what they are and how they are developed and used in an interview.

- **Action Imperatives** – what are they.

- **Pre-interview conversation** – before we talk about the crime.

- **Words Mean things** – Language has power.

- **The power of Human Compassion and Human Touch**

- **Push Lines** – Moving the conversation to confession

I'll give you a definition and an example to flesh out these concepts. As we go on you will recognize them in the techniques Ill share.

COGNITIVE DISSONANCE

The next concept is **cognitive dissonance**. In short it is a compound word that means cognitive, or thinking, and dissonance or confusion or disturbance. When a person's thoughts are disrupted, as in an alibi, or during an interview, they can become confused and lose the ability to maintain any lies they were telling you. They will change their stories to overcome their confusion. The confusion usually comes when you present them with facts that don't fit their narrative or alibi.

If you are interviewing a person who committed a robbery and they are giving you their story about being nowhere near the convenience store at the time of the robbery, you could ask a follow up such as:

Officer: *"Were you at that store at any time that day?"*

For the most part the suspect might not expect that question, this could cause them some confusion or cognitive dissonance which you can see in their facial expressions, in their body language and in the words that come out of their mouths. By asking this question you may have upset the predetermined lie they wanted to tell you, they now have to consider that question and answer properly.

It has been my experience that many suspects will want to avoid placing themselves at the crime scene for any reason and they will tell you:

Suspect: *"No", I was not there at all.*

Once you get that answer you might follow it up with:

Officer: *Are you sure you were not there at all today? Did you stop in for coffee on the way to work?*

Here is where they have to make another choice and alter the story they wanted to tell you, it will also make them consider why you are asking that question. This can cause a bit of cognitive dissonance.

Suspect: *No, I wasn't there at all today, I told you that.*

By asking this question, then following it up as I showed you, does two things. First it provides more for the suspect to consider as they lie which increases cognitive dissonance that you can see, number two, it locks them in to an answer that is not ambivalent, they told you definitively on two specific instances they were not in the store at all. If this is on video you have an edge now, everyone will hear the questions, the follow up and the answer.

If you have surveillance video from the victim store or a neighboring store that shows the suspect in the area or going into the store, I might hold onto that for a bit and let the suspect lay out their alibi, then when you spring that fact on them it will totally disrupt their thought pattern and cognitive dissonance will be on display. They will have to alter their story, change their memory, or add to their lie to cover the video footage of them in the store. Either way they will have trouble here which you can see as deception and move in for more questions and heat up the cognitive dissonance; anyone watching the interview video will see the suspects changes in story and their lie.

What if you do not have surveillance footage?

While we know we cannot or should not fabricate evidence, such as holding up a surveillance video and saying, "this is the tape from the store showing you inside today", but we know we can tell them something like:

Officer: *"You know that store next to the convenience store has video surveillance and its shows both front doors. What would you say if you are seen on the video footage, we have detectives checking the video right now?"*

Unless the suspect is very familiar with the victim store and knows there is no surveillance cameras, they will have to consider the fact that they are on tape going into the victim store when they just told you they were not there.—**Cognitive Dissonance**. Understanding this concept of cognitive dissonance and how to use it in your interview will help you identify deception in the person you are interviewing.

The physical and verbal responses to cognitive dissonance that you can see can include:

- Stammering

- Sentences that break up

- Rambling as if they were trying to come up with something to say

- Looking away from you and avoiding eye contact

- Hand wringing, shaking toe or finger tapping.

A good example of cognitive dissonance that might be more familiar to many of us from our personal lives and could go something like this:

You tell your significant other you're going out for the evening with a group of friends to watch a sporting event at the local bar. You say you will be home around midnight. While you are out you and your friends decide to leave the sporting event and go to the local exotic dance club. While you are there a very attractive young bartender finds out that you are a group of police officers and starts to tell you about her problematic relationship with her boyfriend and the domestic violence she has suffered.

You being a good person start to give her advice on how she can protect herself. It is very flattering to have this attractive young woman speaking to you. Now you have done nothing wrong engaging in this conversation. But you probably do not want to go home and tell your significant other that you engaged in it as it could be misinterpreted and cause you a problem.

As the evening wears on the young bartender tells you that her boyfriend has sometimes showed up in the parking lot as she was going home and has assaulted her. It is at this time that you realize it is now almost 1:30 in the morning you are way past the time you told your significant other you would be home. This young bartender then asks you to walk her to the parking lot to make sure the boyfriend isn't there, being a good person, you do that, you walk her to her car, she gets in and drives away.

You now drive home to your house. When you arrive at home, had you gotten home at midnight as you said you would have you might just walk in the door very relaxed and prepared yourself for bed. But knowing not only are you late, but you engaged in conversation with a very attractive young bartender, you walked her to her car, and that is why you are so late in returning home even though you did all of that you did not do anything wrong, but many of us would feel uncomfortable telling our significant other this entire story.

Many of us would then instead, quietly enter the house, quietly work our way to the bed hoping to get under the sheets and go to sleep and have the night come to an end.

So imagine yourself tiptoeing into your room, sliding under your covers, and just as you were about to go to sleep the light switch flicks on and your significant other is sitting up and asking you what happened, where were you, and why are you so late? What do you say? Do you blurt out the truth or say something else?

This little tale is something many people can identify with, and I bring it up because I want you to think about being that person, how would you feel at that moment when the light switch clicked on and you were asked that question and know you have to come up with a reasonable answer that didn't put you in a position of awkward discomfort. We might be confused we might be unsure what to say, we might start to babble as we answer in an effort to respond and seem credible. That is cognitive dissonance, we were caught off guard and we were concerned about what to say, we don't want to cause ourselves a problem, but we have to say something. This is how suspects often react when you interview them and add new information that disturbs their planned story or alibi.

The reason cognitive dissonance causes so many problems for people is because of our next concept—**Jeopardy**.

JEOPARDY

Next, we need to understand Jeopardy and how it affects human beings and how they respond and react.

Jeopardy is defined as a situation where you have something to lose, there are potential consequences at stake, you might suffer a loss, you might be convicted of a crime and go to jail. Jeopardy is serious and it can make human beings react very strongly to whatever develops the jeopardy.

In our case as law enforcement investigators when we interview a suspect their jeopardy is most often centered around being charged with a crime, being prosecuted, paying fines, or going to jail or prison. There are other potential items of jeopardy that could cause a person to be concerned such as embarrassment, loss of trust, loss of status or loss of respect from others they value.

If we think of our late-night homecoming event described earlier, from the facts presented he really did nothing wrong, but we know our significant other may be hurt by our actions, they may feel betrayed or they may think we lied. Any of those things can cause us a great deal of personal and relationship pain, so most people would not mention it and hope for the best to avoid any jeopardy.

If we compare the jeopardy of the convenience store robber and the late-night coming home guy, we can see the different types of jeopardy each could feel, I break them down into two categories, one is criminal, the other is personal.

Understanding what potential jeopardy a suspect faces, either genuinely or in their perception, criminal or personal, can help you tailor your interview to enhance the feelings of jeopardy to induce cognitive dissonance and an opportunity for you to identify deception, dishonesty or guilt.

Using jeopardy to induce cognitive dissonance is where practice comes in. We don't always want to make a suspect's options so terrible, sometimes we want to offer them a way out or a way to assuage their negative feelings in the case of a person with personal jeopardy.

We need to see the differences between personal and criminal jeopardy and where they can come into play in an investigation.

Criminal Jeopardy is the easiest, a person commits a crime and they don't want to get arrested, charged or go to jail it is pretty simple.

The person with Personal Jeopardy may be involved in a criminal investigation, but their jeopardy is not because they committed a crime, it can be because they engaged in activities that may be morally wrong, or embarrassing and they can be deceptive during an interview because they don't want their behavior to come to light.

An example might be at a workplace, a woman engages in an affair with a co-worker. This is against company rules and she is married. At the same time money has been stolen from a safe in the business where she works and as you interview the employees, she comes across as deceptive when asked about timelines and where she was during the workday, what rooms she was in and who she was with. She is not involved in the theft, but her body language, facial expressions and answers can all look like deception and criminal jeopardy when in reality they are due to her personal jeopardy.

I make this point so that when you are looking at an individual or a group of suspects you recognize that you must not jump to conclusions based on old style police theory or TV detective's techniques. You have to understand what motivations people have in any given incident and where their jeopardy comes from. You will do this by being curious and asking the right questions.

Cognitive Dissonance and Jeopardy go hand in hand, they are powerful concepts that can help guide you and help you decipher what people say and why. In the coming chapters you will see how they are intertwined in all parts of interview technique.

POSSIBILITIES

Possibilities are what we call a series of potential excuses that you, the interviewer, covertly suggest to the suspect during the interview process to help the suspect explain their actions during an incident that makes their actions seem more acceptable. Since most people who have committed some type of crime may not want to admit to it right away, we have to understand that in their mind any admission is a problem.

Possibilities then are more acceptable reasons for a person's action, a reason that is more societally acceptable. Such as a person stealing bread and milk to feed their kids is still stealing, but most people can understand why a person would do such a thing. It softens the blow of the crime. We offer the suspect these possibilities so they can admit to their actions with an acceptable excuse.

The purpose of these Possibilities is to encourage the suspect to admit involvement in a crime or incident for reasons other than the truthful reasons they committed the act. You give them more acceptable motives they can admit to by giving the other "Possible" reasons for their actions other than criminal.

Possibilities, described at their most basic, are things we can identify in our conversation with our suspect or subject that are important to them, have some meaning for them or are a concern for them. They are topics such as family, friends, jobs, relationships, achievements or disappointments, tragedies, challenges, joys, or burdens. We want to identify these possibilities so we can use them at key moments in our conversations with a person to elicit more conversations, stir emotions, or create a compelling moment.

Possibilities are alternative motives the suspect can latch onto to explain their criminal behavior in a way that sounds more acceptable and plausible so they can explain their behavior and avoid responsibility and punishment.

We use possibilities to sometimes help the suspect create an excuse for their actions using the things going on in their lives. We get the possibilities by listening to the suspect when we talk about family, friends, jobs etc.

When engaged in an interview with a purpose such as a criminal interview, we have to use all of the tactics and techniques of a chess match. We are interacting in real time, but we must consider where we want the conversation to go, how we can get there, and what we can use to help us. Possibilities do just that.

As an example: if a woman kills her husband for insurance money, it is reasonable to assume that she knows this is murder for profit and she will be treated very severely in the court system. It is also a good bet she will not just simply confess to her crime and tell you the terrible truth of why she killed him; for the money. However, a skilled interviewer knows this reality and will offer some alternative possibilities to the suspect to explain her actions so that she can mitigate her real criminal behavior.

What I might say to this suspect is something like this:

"I know that in many marriages there are hidden things that go on behind closed doors. Not every husband is a great guy, some husbands can be outwardly wonderful but brutal when no one is looking. Did you and your husband have any problems like that?"

This Possibility is obvious. I am asking the suspect to jump on the "Yes he hit me, and I was just protecting myself" band wagon. She might see this as a reasonable excuse for shooting her husband, accept it, and then fabricate her story to match that reasonable and acceptable possibility.

In the suspect's mind the possibility provides her with some cover for her actions, cover that may not look like criminal behavior or can explain away criminal behavior.

Remember, during the initial part of our interview, we don't care why they put themselves at the scene of the crime committing an illegal action, the goal is to get them to admit being there and doing something. Further conversation between you and the suspect will bring out the truth. Even if they refuse to tell you anything but their concocted story, your investigation, along with the physical evidence and other statements will prove what actually happened.

ACTION IMPERATIVES

Demanding that people tell us the truth or give any other information for that matter is a fool's errand. Bullying someone in an interview rarely works and can in fact be an alienating tactic that causes them to resist talking or throw out the dreaded *"Can I talk to a lawyer?"*

Demands like this are known as **action imperatives**. An action imperative is a demand for someone to do something. In police work we use them all the time; you will recognize them—

- Get out of the car.

- Put your hands on your head.

- Shut up/don't talk.

- Get your hands out of your pockets.

- Come over here.

We use action imperatives in police work to exert control over a situation, person or scene. Action imperatives have their place in police work; however, in an interview they can be, and usually are, detrimental to obtaining a confession to anything.

I often think of a young police officer at the scene of a domestic disturbance where the husband had retreated to the bedroom when the patrols arrived. He refused to come out and the officer was getting annoyed. To deal with his annoyance the officer turned to action imperatives—"Come out now or you're going to jail for 20 years!"

If you heard that comment would you come out?

No, I wouldn't either. So, we see that action imperatives can cause problems and should be avoided at all cost, if possible.

WHAT ARE ACTIVE LISTENING SKILLS?

Good question. Active listening skills means we need to use our ears as much as our mouths in an interview. For most people in any given situation, especially a conversation with another person, criminal or otherwise, when there's a lull in the talk they think they have to fill it up with words. Wrong.

We must listen to what the person is saying, what words they are using, what emotions you hear in their comments and what their body language is telling you. The best way to get important information is often to just listen—be quiet and listen to the suspect, victim or witness.

There will be more on Words Means Things later in the book, but the concept of Active Listening means to hear what the other person is saying, directly or indirectly.

A common communication problem for humans, and one that has been put into a little saying by author Stephen R. Covey, is—"Most people do not listen with the intent to understand; they listen with the intent to reply."

This saying is filled with value for the interviewer and makes a clear point. If we are listening only so we can prepare a response, we will miss a lot of valuable information.

A real-life example of this Active Listening Dynamic can be found in the work of a car salesperson ... believe it or not.

A car salesperson's job is to overcome your denials and get you to buy the car and up sell you if they can. Your job is to leave the car lot with the exact car you want and need at a price you can afford to pay; you don't want to leave with a huge car loan for a car you didn't really want. You both have a vested interest in the interaction and the outcome. Both sides have tactics.

The salesperson listens to what you say as you engage in car chitchat such as: What colors do you like, how many doors so you want, what size motor, and what style? What they won't talk about is the price. What's actually going on here is the salesperson is gathering intel on you and by discovering what's important to you, he/she wants to play to your ego if possible; for instance, suggesting a sports car instead of a family sedan at twice the cost. They want to listen to your life situation and see how they can use that information against you as the sales pitch goes forward, especially when you try to move the deal in your favor or leave all together.

A fact about sales pitches in the U.S. is that statistically 8 out of 10 people cannot say NO during a sales negotiation. Salespeople know this, and it works to their advantage. The salesperson wants to find out what bait works for you and then play that up to drive you toward the sale. They give you some line to run out and eventually convince you to buy the most expensive car she can put you in. You might find that the salesperson's schtick will change as you put up a strong fight and resist the sales pitch. Therefore, the "Best car ever made and is perfect for you" might morph into "Yeah, maybe not the best choice, let me show you something else that will be perfect." His reality will shift as the deal moves away and he tries to salvage it. Same thing happens in an interview. If you listen for these subtle changes in details and the storyline presented by your suspect, you can be confident as you work the interview that they are hiding information.

In most cases, the best-prepared person usually wins the interaction. Because most people can't say no, a salesperson will keep asking questions to get you to say "Yes," such as: *"You said you want a two-door car, right?"* "Yes." *"You said you love bright red, right?"* "Yes." *"You said you would love to get the leather and V-8 if the price was right, correct?"* "Yes."

The salesperson uses all the elicited information from you and uses it to condition you to say "Yes." This is a sales technique that combines knowledge of human nature and talking skills. He/she wants to move you to their objective through conversation and questions backed with facts while using your info against you. This usually leads to the following final question:

"If I can get you the V-8, two-door with leather, in bright red, at your price would you buy it today?" (Most people feel cornered

when all their objections are overcome, and their will is overrun.) "Yes," you say. BAM! Car salesman - 1, you - 0. A good salesperson guides the conversation where they want it to go.

Our job as investigators and interviewers is to get the suspect to come our way and give up the truth. We do it the same way, there's a game plan, techniques, information and skill.

So, *where do we find the right bait in an interview?*

MORE ABOUT POSSIBILITIES

Here is where one of our key terms comes into play— "Possibilities." The salesperson uses casual conversation to identify things you find important, or desirous in a car such as , style, color, engine size horsepower etc. Then during the sales pitch, he/ she uses them to move you towards the sale by combining a knowledge of what you see as important with knowledge of human nature and getting you to say yes. Before you know it, you're in the finance office signing up for a beautiful, but more expensive car then you set out to buy. These possibilities are the "BAIT."

We find our possibilities in the same casual conversation when we talk with suspects during the **pre-interview conversation.**

PRE-INTERVIEW CONVERSATION AND SETTING A BASELINE FOR RESPONSES.

To understand the value that the Pre-interview conversation has to the overall success of an interview we have to understand the concept and mind set of many people when they are interviewed. As I cover this you will see how several of these concepts begin to converge.

Most people are nervous around the police, especially if they are in the police station, that's natural. If they have done something wrong or illegal, their intensity will be even higher because they have greater Jeopardy. We use this fact to help us evaluate the persons words and body language so we can make a call on whether they are being deceptive or truthful.

During the pre-interview conversation we can present ourselves in such a way as to begin to develop a bond with the person we are going to interview. We should not be aggressive we should be calm and relaxed. Do not dive right into asking about the crime or incident. The suspect expects this and has their guard up, so you do the opposite talk about other things- Sports, family, jobs, kids, parents, hobbies, your favorite beer, or anything else besides the crime or incident under investigation. Think of what you would talk about if you just met someone at a party or bar. You would just be talking general stuff.

This pre-interview conversation can help calm the suspect, help them to see you as less of a threat (Not a physical threat, but a threat to their freedom, this is their jeopardy). When the suspect or anyone you have to interview calms down and feels less jeopardy you can see their natural conversational style, how they really speak and react when talking.

You want to watch for their reactions once they have calmed down and you talk about general things of life. Based on this general conversation you want to pick up on things they have an interest in that is not connected to the crime or the incident you are investigating. As an example, the suspect is wearing a NY Yankees tee shirt. You mention it's a cool shirt and ask if he/she likes the Yankees. They say yes, it's their favorite team. This is great you have a topic to talk about that they are interested in.

So, there you are talking about the NY Yankees, the players, the team's record, the chances of going to the world series. The suspect is engaged, relaxing a bit, and showing you a bit of who they are in real life.

As you ask questions and talk you want to see how they react to this relaxed conversation when there is no jeopardy. Do they look you in the eye when you talk, do they answer quickly without hesitation, can they recall facts about the team from several years ago, are they sitting up, smiling, laughing, leaning forward and showing interest in what you have to say?

That is a normal conversational speech pattern. Your goal here is to see these normal, non-stressed reactions of words and body language when there is no jeopardy.

Knowing how they react here gives you a good baseline for their non-jeopardy responses. This baseline is what you will use to compare to their reactions of words and body language when you transition to the actual interview talking about the crime or incident under investigation.

The Takeaway from the concept of setting a baseline for your suspects reactions.

When we see a person is calm and not concerned about the jeopardy they face, you will see them look you in the eye when they talk, arms are down not crossed, they engage easily. They have fast recall of facts and their spoken sentences are complete and understandable.

When jeopardy is presented by moving onto the questions about the crime or incident under investigation you will see a marked change in their behaviors.

They may tense up, cross their arms or legs, repeat questions back to you, seem confused, think too long to respond. They may show disinterest in what you are talking about. You might hear their spoken sentences come out as broken, chopped up or disjointed. They may fade in an out as they try to figure out what is the best way to answer your questions to alleviate their jeopardy.

All of these things can be seen very easily once you have set a baseline for how the person reacts, so take your time with the pre- interview conversation and pay attention.

REFER back to these definitions as we go forward. You will see how they interplay with one another and others we will cover.

WORDS MEAN THINGS. LANGUAGE HAS POWER.

Human beings communicate in many ways, with body language (80%) and with verbal language. Therefore, the words, the tone of voice, the way we use the words in connection with body language we use can have a huge impact on how we transfer information between human beings. Remember the saying by Steven Covey, "The problem with communication is that people listen to respond they don't listen to understand." This tells us that making sure the message you are sending is the message you intend to send. The words we use as people is the vehicle for delivering that message.

This is one of the four (4) techniques I offer. This one is called "Diminishing" and it is very powerful. It is a use of words technique. By diminishing the descriptions of certain parts of the crime we convey a message to the person being interviewed that it is not as bad as it seems. We make the impact of the words less to help prevent the suspects Jeopardy from rising too high.

An example: A person reports a sexual assault, a terrible violation of another person. If you are talking to the suspect and say you are investigating an accusation that they "Raped" someone, that message will scream: "YOU are going to JAIL," but if you diminish the words, the impact is softened. You might say "A person says you had sex with them."

The difference in the words is obvious. Having sex with someone is not a frightening as the word Rape, therefore your suspect will have a lesser sense of jeopardy.

This concept is used over and over and is a key to getting confessions and admissions. Words have power use them correctly.

More on "Words Mean Things" later—it's that important.

THE POWER OF HUMAN COMPASSION AND HUMAN TOUCH

An interview can be a very intimate encounter with another person. Not all interviews are, job interviews for example don't lend themselves to intimacy, they are more straight forward. They can be friendly or aggressive, but not usually connective.

Criminal interviews on the other can be an intimate interaction. Don't confuse intimate with a sexual experience, that's not the intimacy I mean. I am referring to the fact that in a criminal interview we are dealing with things that people did that they know are wrong, they know were violent, or imposed pain on another human being. Other than a sociopath who has no concern for the feelings of others, most people can find revealing their terrible deeds, thoughts, feelings, and beliefs to another person very emotional. Confessing can trigger a lot of responses of remorse, sadness, fear, or shock at one own behavior when forced to confront what they did to another person.

We are dealing with human beings who are made up of thoughts and feelings. When we are interacting with those thoughts and feelings it can be like a swirling storm of emotion. Harnessing that reality and using that knowledge can give you an advantage in an interview as you lead a person to confess.

When people are faced with their own actions and behavior's they can sometimes try very hard to ignore what they have done for reasons other than just simple jeopardy and the consequences of their actions. Robbing a liquor store with no violence other than maybe the threat to do violence will elicit a jeopardy response in the suspect. They know they didn't hurt anyone but robbing a store usually means jail time.

When a suspect has done a violent thing to another person that can be a bigger psychological problem for them. An adult male who sexually assaults a child for their own sexual pleasure may do so by blocking those thoughts from their mind especially if they did the act without physical force. If they coerced or fooled the child into the activity, but if actual physical force was used on a crying victim or one that struggled or put up resistance to the assault, that can be very painful to confront during an interview when forced to face their actions. Same is true for any violent act committed against another person.

Understanding these emotional aspects of what a person has done can help you guide the conversation and use these feelings to move a person to confess and repent.

That sounds religious doesn't it? Well, think about it, what is the purpose of confession in a religious setting? It is to assuage your guilt, obtain forgiveness, and cleanse your soul.

This works in a religious setting because most people have a built in need to confess when they do a bad thing, its part of our human nature (Except for sociopath's). If we understand this reality about human nature it can work in an interview setting as well. Most people have need to confess once caught, but they fight it because of the consequences this will face. These two forces are always at battle. Knowing this can help you as you work the interview.

With this background in place, how does this knowledge of human compassion help you in an interview?

When a person is feeling down, scared, alone, or guilty it can be very isolating. If you have built any kind of a bond with the person you may be able to offer some comfort to them when these feelings come forward. If you set the stage correctly, when you break through the denials and get to the responsibility part of the process, they may feel all alone facing the consequences of their actions (Personal regret) or jeopardy (Legal consequences). When you extend them compassion it can bond them to you and create an environment where you become very important to them for forgiveness of what they did (They believe you know their really not evil they did something stupid or bad) or you can help mitigate their consequences (You can tell the court they made mistakes, they are sorry, you are a voice for them).

Here's where many investigators find a problem. How do you show compassion to a person who has done a terrible thing to another person? Who would want to show compassion to that person?

This is where you need to come to terms with your job and your duties. You must understand that if you do not get the confession the person who did this terrible thing might go free and the victim will not receive justice. That is a huge responsibility on your part, and it takes effort to create this place in your own head to do this work. It can be emotional for you too.

I managed to create this place in my head by understanding my responsibility in the justice system. I could not let my personal feelings as a human being dictate how I did my work, if I did, I would not have been able to deal with some of the people I had to deal with. People who had done unspeakable things to other people. In time I came to see my work as vital to the system and being a part of the process to bring justice for victims and protect society from evil people. Sounds grandiose, but isn't it really true, isn't that what we do in law enforcement? Yes, it is. And sometimes to do our work we have to go to places we would not choose otherwise. We have to connect to bad dangerous and evil people to do what needs to be done. It is not always pleasant, but if you get your head right, you can do wonders for good people.

This work is not for everyone, that's OK to say and for anyone of us to admit. It can be ugly, and it can be emotionally painful. This is one of the reasons law enforcement officers commit suicide at such high rates, while on the job and years after retirement. The emotional realities of seeing human pain and suffering takes its toll on many of our brothers and sisters. This is why you must look inside yourself and ask the hard questions. Can you do this for the greater good.

It is not easy, but I can say, once I put this work in its own place, I sleep like a baby. You can too.

The next part of this concept of Human Compassion is the Power of Human Touch.

Important—Touching anyone must be done appropriately.

To get this concept you have to feel the concept personally. So, lets all think of a time you met someone you really liked romantically. Do you remember the excitement of the first meeting, the anticipation of the first date, the tingling when you saw them? All of these emotions create a chemical reaction in your body because the mind and body are connected. You might have felt euphoria when just thinking of the person.

Now let's move to the first time you were with that person and you touched their hand. For many of us it was electric, you could literally feel the spark when your hands touched and grasped, it was very powerful. This is built into the human system, we are built to react this way to other people, it keeps the species alive.

We can use this knowledge of human interaction in our interviews and encounters with a suspect or witness.

Let's go back to the suspect who is defeated, but not yet confessed. We know they are feeling many emotions, maybe disgust of their actions, remorse, sadness, and fear of consequences. They are isolated in their jeopardy.

You use push lines and compassion to get to them and at the right moment placing a hand on a shoulder or arm can create the same spark of connection that people feel when they connect romantically, even though this connection is NOT romantic. It is still a powerful connection to a person who is in need and if they are bonded to you in any way it can move them very strongly.

I have had hardened criminals break down and cry at this moment of the interview. I have had them confess and then hug me and thank me for taking their statement, a statement that will put them in prison for many years. The power of human compassion and human touch can sometimes overcome the fear of their jeopardy. Use it carefully and wisely, it is a game changer.

PUSH LINES—MOVING CONVERSATION TO CONFESSION

A Push Line is a term I use to describe a specific set of words you say to a suspect or witness to move them towards an admission or confession. When I say "Push" it does not mean to do so forcefully or physically, it means a psychological push.

As you conduct your interview you may see signs that subject is weakening in their denials of involvement or knowledge about an incident or crime. You may see signs that they cannot continue to resist the logic of your evidence or facts about the incident or crime and their involvement in it, but they still cannot bring themselves to confess.

The signs you might see are verbal and physical (Body Language). They may speak slower, they may sound defeated, they may slump their shoulders or look down at the table or floor, they might seem depressed. If they had been very aggressive in their denials this change will be obvious. It is natural for a person to show these signs of defeat when they realize they are not winning the conversation, that the interview has led to the only place it could, their guilt.

Even at this point the desire of self-preservation (Preventing the jeopardy) may be strong enough for them to know its over but not to accept it. We use "Push Lines" to help them over the finish line.

An example:

A robbery suspect initially denied any knowledge of the crime. They denied being at the scene, they denied robbing anyone. As your interview progressed and you took apart their alibi or story, you used your evidence and other statements and persuasion to paint a very clear picture of their involvement. You rebutted everything they came up with to deny their participation and now they sit looking defeated, depressed, tired, and maybe scared of the consequences of their actions (Their Jeopardy). You add some push lines to move them:

"Bob look, we have been talking for 2 hours about this mess (diminishing the robbery word), I've gotten to know a little bit about you and I know you are not a bad person, (Building a bond). I heard you tell me about your mom who is not healthy and needs very expensive medicines (Possibilities), I get it, I have a mom too that I love and would do anything for. The way I see it you were pushed pretty hard to do something to help her get that medicine, I think you did something stupid (Diminishing). I think you did something that if you could have done another way you would have. (Pause here, maybe reach out and put a hand on his shoulder or arm (Human compassion and bonding). Bob.... Am I right about you, you're not a bad guy, you're a desperate guy, (Possibility) a desperate guy that did something he should not have done?

This type of conversation shows how push lines are used in connection with other techniques we have already covered like diminishing and the power of human compassion and touch and how to use it.

In many instances, when a suspect is defeated and ready to confess, push lines can be the thing that takes them over the thresh hold into the land of confession. It is critical that you have developed a bond, even a limited bond and you use the push lines in a genuine fashion. If you thought of yourself as a counselor helping someone through a problem that is the tone you use.

Push line can be very powerful. And when you are on camera, can be devastating to a defense attorneys attack on you as less than caring or appropriate. Watching the suspect break and confess after using Push lines correctly can be very emotional for a jury. The important point here is that they confessed. This emotional response can create a bond for everyone, they jury included who will see you as compassionate and may see the suspect as a sympathetic figure, but they will be connected.

Chapter 3 - The Interview Starts Off

PROPER GREETINGS

With every interview there is a starting point. That might be out in the street, on the phone, in headquarters or at the crime scene. We want to start off on our best foot so to speak. Remember, building a bond is what connects people together, even during the short time of an interview. This bond will allow you to elicit information from the suspect or witness they might not ordinarily give. During this initial meeting how we treat the person to be interviewed and how they perceive us will set the groundwork of the encounter.

Start off with: Professional Greeting

- A respectable, professional tone

- Make eye contact

- A good handshake, not a vice grip or a soft hand.

- Introduce yourself by title: I'm detective Jones, I'm investigator Smith, I'm patrol officer Gleason, I'm Correctional Officer Hodgkins, I'm Sergeant Wilson. Etc.

- Ask their name: I'm Dan Carter.

- Ask if you can call them by their first name. First names are more intimate than titles or Mr./ Mrs. This starts the bonding process. When you meet a new person out in the world, we usually use first names after the introduction, its natural. If the suspect says you can use their first name offer yours.

Understand this:

Many people who are involved in crime or who have had police contacts may not be used to being treated professionally or respectfully. When you do these things, you create a new paradigm for them: The cop not as an enemy, but as a person.

This is especially true if the arrest was difficult. If they resisted or had some other negative experience. You may want to address any injuries they have right away, even if they have already received first aid. It shows concern, which builds bonds.

You might also offer a drink or food depending on the circumstance. When we "break bread" with people it is a connecting time. I often offered coffee or soda to suspects.

If the suspect complains to you about the arrest you can use this opportunity to distance yourself from the arrest incident and the officers who arrested the suspect. I have had suspects tell me the "Cops beat me up". This can be a difficult position to be in, but address it, but control the way you address it.

There are legitimate uses of force, but the suspect might not always agree, so I would say something like this: I'm sorry that happened to you, our PD has a very strict use of force policy. No one wants anyone to get hurt. I'll make sure I tell the sergeant and they will look into your complaint."

Sometime this is enough to let the suspect move past the incident for the moment. It also shows you are concerned for them.

While this concern for the suspect might seem unnecessary, or unwarranted especially if they were resisting arrest never forget your mission—To get an admission, or a confession. The bigger picture has to guide you. If the suspect was injured due to an inappropriate action by an officer, it will be investigated and should be. Use this opportunity to connect to the suspect to get the admission or confession.

We do what we have to do within the legal boundaries we have to get an admission or confession. If showing concern for the suspect, even a pretend concern works, then you do it.

Once you have gotten past the initial introduction and you set the stage for the interview to begin you must be ready mentally and physically for the task ahead.

Your job at this point in the interview is to throw out possibilities to your suspect. Possibilities to explain his actions and so forth. Give him some choices. Does he have an alcohol or drug problem? Is he trying to feed his hungry kids, is he taking care of a dying parent? Mostly that's B.S., but you have to understand the suspect's mind set. If he is your guy, he is the one who committed the crime, he most likely will want to avoid taking responsibility for his actions. The people who just fold and roll over and confess are not your problem. Those cases are easy and take care of themselves. I am concentrating on the guys/gals who don't give it up. The ones who make you work for it. Career criminals, those who have done jail time and don't fear it, street smart people who have gotten over before, intelligent suspects who think they are smarter than you. The tactic of throwing out possibilities gives the suspect a chance to rationalize his actions, behavior or presence at a crime scene without saying he did anything wrong. That is a huge part of our goal, and one of the first obstacles we must get past—to get the suspect to put himself at the scene.

A classic interview might go like this:

Cop: "So Bill, I know you would never actually rob an old woman."

Bad Guy: "Of course not, man!"

Cop: "I'm thinking that there has to be some reason that she said it was you and you are on the store video."

This is where our criminal suspect starts thinking "How do I explain this?" You want to give him a reason that sounds plausible but still does not mean he is guilty of a crime. That will come later. Give him some possibilities!

Cop: I know, I've checked your record, you don't have any violence in it. I'm thinking that this is a big mistake. The woman dropped the purse and you picked it up to give to her and she panicked thinking you were stealing it so you took off. Is that close to what happened, is that possible?"

This line of reasoning gives the suspect something to grasp onto. If he knows he's on the videotape, then he knows he has to explain his presence there at some point. Giving him this "Plausible Possibility" reason makes it more comfortable for him to say he was there and he did touch the purse, albeit for a good reason. The goal of your questioning here is to get the suspect to put himself at the scene. Once he does that you can begin to work on his story and move him off the "Good" story you helped him to bite into and move him toward the truth of his actions. It's a process, it takes time and patience.

The days of yelling and screaming in an interview are long gone. But I want to be clear here, those tactics never really worked any way, and anyone who tells you they did, has no idea how to conduct a proper interview to begin with. The force at work in an interview that leads to confessions is building a bond of trust and respect between yourself and the suspect. It is your job to help the suspect see that their best chance of mitigating their actions is through the relationship with you. That does not mean that you will be best friends or see each other socially at holidays. What it does mean is that the suspect will come to see you as their ally and believe that by telling you what they did (or at least a facsimile of what they did), they can achieve their best chance of leniency.

This is something you will want to foster, BUT... never lie to a suspect about what you can or cannot do for them. Many a good cop has gone down this road only to see their case shot to hell because they made a promise to a suspect as to what sentence they would get or what bail or lack of it they could arrange if the suspect told the truth. What we can do is let the suspect know that we will make their cooperation and truthfulness and sense of remorse known to the prosecutor, judge, and others, which is perfectly fine, but no more. If you have handled the suspect properly, showed him/her respect and some compassion, then you will not have to make promises in the first place.

PROMISES

Let's talk about making promises and why it's a problem. First, we are the good guys and good girls of law enforcement, we don't lie about what we can do for someone, that would be unfair and if you can't do what you said, it can be cruel. Second, promising someone you will do something to induce them to confess or admit their involvement in a crime or incident can result in false confessions, or made up facts to convince you that the person is sincere since you're going to help them. Third, we are law enforcement personnel. We investigate, we arrest, we charge, we are part of the prosecution team offering evidence of our investigations. We Are NOT the prosecutors. The prosecutors or District Attorneys run the trials and make any deals or plea bargains. We all have unique rolls to play in the criminal justice system.

Making a promise to get a confession will be brought up in the trial or in the pre-trial motions and they never look good for us. They give the connotation that we made the promises to get the admissions as a trick or a tool to take advantage of the suspect. We also look like we overstepped our boundaries since the prosecutors make the deals, and no one likes having someone step over the boundary. Imagine if a prosecutor came in and told you how to conduct your investigations? You would not be happy. We all swim in our own lanes so to speak.

And finally, any promises you make will be told to the jury who could very naturally assume we are doing something inappropriate and it can damage your case. *Don't do it.*

What we can do though is tell then suspect that you will convey their cooperation to the prosecutor or judge. This is acceptable, because you are not making any promises you are simply telling the suspect you will make their cooperation, truthfulness as well as any help they provide to you in your investigation known to the people who can make deals and promises about their charges or sentence. This also helps create

a bond between you and the suspect because now they see you as
s someone who can help them – and inside guy or gal kind of
thing.

RESPECT

Be respectful as possible to your suspect or witness.

By revealing your sense of respect for any human being, you
allow others, including the suspect, to reveal theirs. Sounds like
a lot of nonsense, but if you work at it, you will see it works. We
are dealing with people. At our core we are all really the same,
you must get to that person inside the criminal and get the
confession. As I said earlier, many people involved in criminal
activity are not used to a respectful conversation with the
authorities, it is often adversarial due to the nature of the
activities they engage in. By being respectful you can change the
dynamic in your favor.

One problem we all have is that we are the good guys and
good girls. We don't rape and rob and beat innocent people. The
bad guys do. Building a relationship with this person may seem
like the last thing in the world you would want to do, even for a
short time. This kind of thinking is normal, but it will help you to
secure your position as a mediocre investigator. You must rise
above yourself and your personal feelings about what the suspect
did. This is what makes you a professional interviewer. It's not
about you, it's about getting the truth. You must lower your
personal level of disgust with the suspects' actions and evil deeds
and extend yourself. Your reward will be getting this bad person
off the streets so he/she cannot injure anyone else.

In many instances you will get the suspect to admit
wrongdoing, but their true rationale for why they did what they
did will almost always be only a piece of the real reasons for their
crime. Sometimes the inner motivations for their actions are too
horrible to actual say to another person, let alone admit to
themselves. An example of this is the sexual criminal. You may
get this person to admit to having intercourse with a 10-year-old
child, but their reason will be "She looked older, she came onto
me, I had no idea she was 10." That might be all you get from the

suspect. Their true motives might actually be that they are drawn to young children sexually and they wanted to have forced sex with a small child as part of a fantasy they have created for themselves. Getting them to admit this reality though can be very difficult, because even though these types of pedophiles might talk to you, admitting their true desires and motivations is something they know is way out of acceptable norms of human behavior. In other words, they know their behavior is unaccept- able, so they shield it and try to explain the behavior with other more acceptable reasons. One of the first steps is to get the suspect to admit being at the scene of the crime or incident.

Either way, once they admit to being at the scene with the victim and committing the act, you let the evidence join into the story and the jury will be able to piece together the facts and come to the proper conclusion.

As human beings we are susceptible to some terrible and powerful demons. Most of us resist these feelings. Some people do not. They give in to their impulses and do very bad things. Most of us also know when something we did was very bad. We feel guilty about it. The suspect's feeling of guilt is what you will chisel away at like a sculpture until you help the suspect reveal the truth to you. But again, you must remember that sometimes when people give in to their desires, they can and will not admit their real motivations. It is the feeling of guilt that keeps many people from committing acts of crime, it can be powerful if you were raised to believe crime is wrong.

Then there are the psychopaths, sociopaths, and just plain damaged members of our society who would think nothing of killing an old woman and leaving her dead for the $10 in her purse. Good luck here. Fortunately for us there are not many of these types walking around. They are out there, but we don't cross them too often.

WHAT IS A SOCIOPATH?

A definition from Healthline.com provides this description:

> A sociopath is a term used to describe someone who has
> antisocial personality disorder (ASPD). People with ASPD
> can't understand others' feelings. They'll often break rules
> or make impulsive decisions without feeling guilty for the
> harm they cause.
>
> People with ASPD may also use "mind games" to control
> friends, family members, co-workers, and even strangers. They
> may also be perceived as charismatic or charming.

With this kind of person, the sociopath, you will want to
appeal to their sense of power and help them brag about what
they did. You will need to let yourself go in this interview. The
suspect will want to tell you about what he did IF you think what
he did was OK. He will consider telling you about his actions so
you can help him craft the best defense for his actions. This is a
different devil altogether. And the topic of another book someday.
Suffice it to say these types of criminals are not your ordinary bad
guy and you had better be prepared if you come across one.

To sum up an interview you have to be in it for the game,
because that's what it is. They know something, you want to
know something. They don't want to tell; you want them to tell.
Be open to anything that moves the conversation along. Just don't
make promises and remember you are the good guy/girl. Get the
confessions.

Chapter 4 - The Art of Interview—
Why Do I Call it an Art?

DEFINITION

I call it an art because to do it well the interviewer has to understand the concepts of effectively talking to another person and then use those concepts in a skillful way that fosters a conversation where truthful information is exchanged. This requires skill, finesse, and the ability to control the interaction without looking like you are controlling it.

It takes practice to become a good interviewer. You have to constantly ensure that you use the techniques and skills I present to you in every possible instance, because to be good at something it must be used all the time to become second nature.

Like a skilled painter who relies on particular paint strokes or a specific brush to bring out her art, the skilled interviewer will use their knowledge of human nature combined with the specific tactics of effective interviewing to bring out the information they are seeking.

I can tell you from experience that the ability to interview people properly is a skill that can be used in every part of your life, especially in a law enforcement career.

When you think about it, almost every interaction we have with other people is a form of interview, whether it's on a car stop, a domestic call, a crisis, a criminal interview, a social date, or a job interview.

In an interview we are seeking information: we want to know something, learn something, and understand something. It is important that we identify and draw out the important information from a conversation and discard anything that does not have value.

It is through these conversations and interviews that we develop our ideas about what happened and how and who was involved and to what extent.

BONDING

And here is the most important thing you need to master how to do: *The key to effectively getting to the information you need is to build a bond with the other person.*

If you fail to establish that bond you may get some information, but you will not get the whole truth.

I will teach you how to build that bond, then you must practice it.

WHAT IS COVERED

- *Specific words and terms* related to human interaction.

- *How people interact with each other* and how you can use that knowledge to move people to speak to you honestly and openly, thereby revealing information you seek from them.

- *Body language* and the hidden meaning of physical gestures—referred to as nonverbal communications. These nonverbal communication cues can sometimes reveal more truth than the spoken word. It will be up to you to recognize them and interpret them accurately.

- *Building a bond* with the person you are interviewing and using that bond to elicit vital information they might otherwise not tell you.

- *Developing trust* and creating a safe environment for talking.

- *Overcoming denials* and the obstacles people face in telling the truth and how you can bridge that gap.

- *How to examine people's words* to decipher between truth, lies, fiction and reality. Words mean things!

- *Nonverbal communications* and body language to spot vulnerabilities and fabrication in people's stories.

- *Overt vs. Covert responses* to questions and what each means to you and the process.

- *Learn to find the truth* even if it is hidden among lies.

- *Giving Miranda*, the importance of this process.

- *Learn to control* our use of these techniques and our own emotions to prevent eliciting false confessions.

UNDERSTANDING THE DIFFERENCE BETWEEN AN INTERVIEW AND AN INTERROGATION AND WHEN EACH SHOULD BE USED

This is where the Concepts of Interview and Interrogation come into play. If you fail to understand what you are doing and why and what effect these skills can have on other people, you will be incapable of using them properly and you will miss out on a tremendous tool you can use in every part of your career and life.

I spend considerable time outlining and explaining the concepts and giving examples of them to bring the ideas to life so that when you are out in the field conducting your interviews and interrogations you will have specific mental memories to fall back on.

By fully understanding a concept, you can determine if it is working on your subject or if you have to change tactics.

UNDERSTANDING HUMAN NATURE

At its essence police work is a person-to-person business; it is a very intimate connection between people. The interview and interrogation process can be a very powerful and emotional endeavor for both the interviewer and the person being interviewed.

Learning how to control that interaction and using the potential emotional bond that develops can give you the advantage you need to solve even the most difficult cases.

Physical evidence is one of the best things we can have in a criminal case, but there is nothing more powerful than a detailed confession to back up the physical evidence.

We have all seen major, high-profile cases based on rock-solid physical evidence fail because of reasons outside the control of the evidence or the investigator, such as jury nullification or impugning the skill of the forensic investigators that collected it, or in some cases an investigator who makes mistakes.

Playing a riveting interview/interrogation confession on video can be the most powerful piece or evidence of all. Learning how to bring these things together is the key to this training.

This particular book covers the interview process and techniques. Interrogation is a separate though related skill, but the two are like cousins, they are related but completely different. I will cover some of the basic concepts of interrogation, so you understand the differences between the two skill sets, but a more in-depth coverage of interrogation techniques will be covered in a later book.

Many people, including those in law enforcement confuse Interview and Interrogation and use the two words interchangeably. This is a mistake. In this book, we are correctly talking about interviewing, which is, as stated earlier, a give and take, and an exchange of information in which a bond is built between interviewer and suspect to foster trust and the exchange of information. Interrogation on the other hand is a much more aggressive, one-sided approach to a conversation with a suspect.

Interrogation techniques are often used when the interview fails to get the information the investigator wants.

This can happen for several reasons:

- The interviewer did not do a good job, failing to get enough background on the suspect or the crime or crime scene.

- The suspect had a very strong will and was able to maintain their emotional control.

- The evidence might have been lacking and the interviewer was fishing.

- The interviewer didn't have the skills needed to overcome the denials of a suspect with a lot of experience dealing with police and police interviews.

- A bond was not created between the interviewer and the suspect.

Interrogation techniques are used to go beyond an interview. Interrogation is basically the interviewer now refusing to allow the suspect to say anything unless it is about their guilt in an incident. The interrogator is verbally forceful and stops the suspect every time they move away from confessing.

Although it does not involve any physical contact, it can be psychologically draining on the suspect and creates a very tense atmosphere.

Interrogation is usually the last action in a case that requires a confession. Interrogation is hardly ever used first unless it is a critical incident such as the need to find a bomb or a weapon and there is no time to try an interview first.

Chapter 5 - Who Makes a Good Interviewer?

PEOPLE WHO INTERVIEW

Some people are naturally gifted speakers; they seem to say the right things at the right time and make people feel comfortable. Most of us know someone who is easy to talk to, someone we feel safe with, someone we can open up to. This happens because that person can build a bond and trust with us.

This ability might be natural in a particular person but the things they do to elicit those feelings can be identified and learned by the rest of us who aren't as naturally gifted.

By identifying the abilities of these naturally gifted speakers and understanding why they were so effective I became a much better interviewer, and I practiced these skills on every person I came across in a criminal format or anywhere else.

Where I grew up there wasn't much crime. For example, the most outrageous criminal things people did were breaking windows and stealing pumpkins at Halloween. When I became a cop, I worked in a community that did have serious crime and serious criminals: rapists, drug dealers, gang members, burglars and killers. I learned very quickly that I needed to relate to many kinds of people from different backgrounds, religions and races if I was going to be successful.

I knew if I wanted to succeed in law enforcement that I would have to learn to talk to people effectively, especially people who had different backgrounds and life experiences. I made a conscious decision to learn all I could about human nature, people's emotions and how they react to things. I talked to every person I encountered and listened to what they had to say. I asked questions earnestly to get people's impressions of how they saw the world so I could use that information as a road map for my career. You have to be like a computer that records information about people and emotions and stores it for future use in similar situations or to help you decipher what people are saying and why. It's about being curious. People's lives are all different in a thousand ways. If we only see things from our point of view and life experiences, we will miss a great deal of information. Be open to things you don't know or understand and seek to gain understanding.

When I was a new cop, I had no idea the many different ways people lived. I went to calls in people's homes from domestics in low income apartment complexes and in million-dollar homes, sometimes on the same shift. Neither lifestyles were the one I grew up with and it felt strange, but I knew I had to open my eyes and see the similarities I could see and adjust my approach. Over time you can do this, but you must be open to it and recognize the value of it.

CURIOSITY

I wrote a column about the value of a police officer's curiosity. I find that many police officers lack this vital desire to be curious about everything around them. That's OK, but once again, if you want to be a successful criminal investigator and interviewer, I believe being curious is of utmost importance.

To help flesh out this concept of curiosity, I think it's worth 2 minutes of your time to read this article and let the concept rattle around:

> "Curiosity"
> by Lt. Joseph Pangaro
>
> I have been asked by many people over the years what they thought was an essential skill for being a police officer. Was it physical strength, the ability to converse, or is it intelligence?
> Those are all great qualities, and all will be helpful to the person who wants a career in law enforcement, but I believe the most essential thing a person needs to become a successful police officer is a good curiosity.

A police officer responds to a person's call for help or assistance. That help might consist of giving advice or taking a report about a crime that was committed, or even arresting someone for something they have done. These tasks can all be accomplished by anyone with some training and experience gathered over time.

What makes a report taker into a world-class investigator is curiosity.

Of all the great law enforcement people I have met over the years, this one element of their personality, this seemingly simple concern is the thing that led them to really achieving great success.

Why? – A simple word but a very powerful concept.

Why did something happen the way it did? What caused it to happen? Why would someone feel that way? Why would someone do such a thing? What makes a person think that way? These are all questions borne of curiosity.

A good example is the residential burglary. An officer arrives and reviews the scene, then takes the report from the resident. They record how the burglar got into the house, what they took and what damage was caused. If that's the end of the interaction and if it is written up correctly the officer will have done an efficient job.

But is it a great job?

Our police officers should not simply be report takers, they should be investigators, crime fighters and defenders of the community. We should provide them with the best training; training that challenges them to do more than just write down what happened. We want them to find out why and how the incident happened so the next time they go on patrol or respond to a call they can use what they learned in previous incidents to prevent a crime or catch the criminal.

The key to this is curiosity. The officer has to have a desire to understand what makes people tick, how they think and behave so they can be one step ahead of the people that would commit crime and do other bad things. It helps to plan your patrols and choose what areas to spend time in.

Asking why is the most basic step in solving crime and preventing new crimes. Asking why should lead to a second and third and fourth question; each answer adding to the officer's knowledge base and revealing other areas to explore.

Knowing the houses most likely to be burglarized can help an officer look for and find suspicious activities. Interviewing the burglar and finding out that they like to choose houses on corners or with large pieces shrubbery that block the view to the yard is important information.

Knowing where people buy their drugs or how they choose to pick a robbery victim helps the planning for future crime prevention. We get these answers from the people who commit these crimes; but if we are not curious about any of this, we can miss a lot of good information. Information that makes for a successful police career and provides a great service to our communities.

I saw this in action many times. My partners, Chuck and Jeff, were two of the best cops I ever met. They seemed to be able to predict where a thief would strike next, or where they would go to sell their stolen property. If we had a crime spree going on these guys had a plan to find the bad guys and catch them. It seemed like they had a sixth sense, but in reality, it was because they were never satisfied with simply taking a report to document an incident. Instead they wanted to know why it happened, how it happened, how was it planned, what tools were used and on and on.

Watching them solve these crimes and catch the perpetrators was not only professionally satisfying but made for a great day at work and a safer community. I remember asking Jeff one time after we set up a surveillance of a particular neighborhood that was being victimized by a burglar; why are we going to set up on this corner?

Jeff's answer was: "Good question — we choose this block because every burglar I ever talked to told me what they were looking for in a house. When you compare that information to the string of burglaries, we are investigating we simply match up the houses in the area that fit the pattern and we wait. They will come to us."

This tactic was a tremendous tool for us to keep our community safe. In fact, it proved to be so successful that after a series of several burglaries in our town and the surrounding towns Chuck created a plan and a prediction of where and when the crook would strike next.

He ran out ahead of us to get set up and before the rest of the team was even out of headquarters, he radioed in that he spotted the suspect. In short order the guy was under arrest and admitted to 15 burglaries in 4 towns.

All of this was possible because these two cops were curious about how and why people do what they do.

I took this concept to heart and never stopped asking questions.

Curiosity is what makes a good cop into a great cop. It's the POWER OF WHY in Policing.

That article points out some simple things to consider, but curiosity has helped me develop and solve more cases than I would have ever thought possible.... How curious are you?

Doing the Work

After I was transferred to the detective bureau, I was faced with interviewing these serious criminals: rapists, thieves, burglars, drug dealers and murderers.

I learned how to handle myself and develop the skills needed to connect with these people. By watching the officers who were good at it, I took what I saw worked for them and adapted what I learned to my personality.

Some things came naturally, others not so much. It was the things that I was not used to, the words, phrases and even life experiences that I were foreign to me that were the hardest to overcome. But I kept at it; I kept practicing.

Over time I added to my repertoire and experience and became comfortable talking to anyone. It was amazing how I could use these skills to get people to confess, but what was even more amazing was not only getting someone to confess to some horrible crime, but developing such a bond with them during the process that many of them thanked me when we were done.

You can do this as well. It is with that understanding that we will move forward to uncover these tactics and skills and learn to use them in our professional lives to make us better investigators.

I believe that anyone can become a good interviewer if they strive to learn how to do it and they use what they learn with an open mind and are willing to evolve in how they apply what they learn through experience.

Words Mean Things

Here is a little more about words mean things.

Every profession has its own set of concepts, knowledge base and principles.

Here is an important guideline for the interviewer: When talking to people about a crime they may have committed or a serious incident they may have been involved in, the words we use to describe their actions can cause them to put up a barrier and refuse to provide any information; but if done properly, it can allow them to feel safe enough to talk to you to try and explain themselves.

The difference is in the words we use.

The concept of words means things is straightforward and simple. Words are the tools and mechanism we humans have to verbally communicate with each other. We also communicate using nonverbal body language. Of the two, nonverbal body language is often more accurate in gauging a person's intent or feelings, especially when hiding information because body language is not put through the filter of the human brain.

If a suspect on a car stop is talking to you but his eyes keep looking around, we know from experience that although he is answering questions and is seemingly cooperating with us, he may actually be looking for a place or opportunity to escape. This body language gives him away as it is raw and unfiltered. If you learn to read this nonverbal language you can prevent a foot pursuit.

A life lesson- "Joe and Chuck on the street"

When I first got moved to the street crimes unit it was really exciting. I had done plainclothes work before and really liked it, but that assignment was sporadic, I helped the detectives with jobs from time to time, which is where I developed my love of detective work. Doing this kind of work full time was a blast and something I looked forward to every shift. My partner, Chuck

Weinkofsky, was guy who lived in town and grew up in the community. He was smart, street savvy and not afraid to do things differently. This was one of the many reasons we got along so well, more than that we became good friends and really bonded as cops.

One of the tasks we did every day was to gather intel from informants or from the patrols about drug activity in town. We then set up random surveillance on several targets to see if anything was happening. If it was quiet in one place, we moved onto another. One night we stopped a young man about 20 years old. He was suspected of selling ecstasy pills. We sat on his house and followed him around until we saw what looked like a "hand to hand" drug sale in a convenience store parking lot.

We were too far off to stop both of the people involved in the suspect transaction, so we called out the buyer's car to patrols who stopped him a few miles away.

Chuck and I stopped the seller. We got him out of the car and took him to the truck area of this car and engaged him in a roadside interview. It was going well he was cooperating, but we noticed that as we were talking to him, he kept looking around. His eyes went from us, to the side of the road, to the property to the left of the car and back again. We also saw that he was slowly inching his way to the left of the trunk. In a natural response Chuck and I moved our position to keep him between us. This went on for about ten minutes when I could see he was tensing up his body, his stance had changed from leaning on the car trunk to a standing position. Crossed arms to hands at his side. His breathing increased and he seemed very nervous. Every time he moved left, we moved left, he moved right we moved right, then like a bolt out of the blue, this guy looks hard left and makes a run for it into the yard next to where we were stopped.

Chuck and I moved his way and lunged at him, and luckily, we caught his arms and legs and all three of us went down in pile. The guy had a bag with over 150 ecstasy pills in it and $2000 cash on him. In his car were another 500 pills. When we got to HQ and interviewed him, we asked what he was thinking at the car stop. He told us very honestly that he knew he had the drugs and he knew we would find them, so he was trying to decide what to do; he was sizing us up to determine if he could get away and if we could catch him. Unfortunately for him he might have had us by 15 years but we were in pretty good shape and even though at the time we weren't catching the subtle body language clues that he was thinking of running, we picked up on it naturally and repositioned ourselves without thinking about it.

That was a great lesson for us and one we never forgot. After that experience we positioned ourselves in better tactical places during roadside interviews. Body language and words make a powerful combination if you know what to look for.

We can also learn to interpret people's intentions and potential actions by learning how words are used to manipulate, twist, or cover a person's meanings, intentions or desires.

If you go on a call to a private residence for a disorderly 25-ear-old man who was fighting with his father, you might hear that the son is "Locked in his room and won't come out," or maybe "He's acting crazy." These two simple phrases can have a lot of meanings. It can be he just doesn't want to come out of his room and deal with the hassle of the cops. A knock on the door and a request to come out and talk will usually work to get the young man out of the room.

But if you try properly, for instance, and he resists by putting things in front of the door to block you, he can actually be a barricaded person, which as we know in police work is a potentially dangerous situation.

Similarly, a person "acting crazy" can be nothing more than a person who is frustrated with the situation and they lash out verbally. Or it could be a person who is emotionally disturbed and potentially dangerous.

What we hear from the callers or the non-police observers on the scene are descriptive words, but we know they can have more meanings depending on the context. The lesson here is to listen to what is said, and how it is said, in context to determine the reality. Active Listening skills come in handy here.

Another good example is a man who is depressed. Maybe he lost a job or a spouse or had some other difficult life loss. He tells you "I don't want to do this anymore." What does that mean?

It can mean he doesn't want to deal with the pain of his situation anymore and he wants to get over it and move on, or it could mean his depression is such that he is suicidal, and he wants to die.

Context combined with conversation can reveal what's really going on. We must listen and pay attention to the words, the tone, and the context to get an accurate understanding of what people really mean by the words they use.

Several years ago, we had a high government official involved in an improper relationship with a young female intern. When that high government official was talking about the situation and answering questions about it, he famously said: "It depends on what is, is."

What the high government official was doing is called parsing his words; he was cutting them up and making their meaning hard to pinpoint. By doing this he was trying to give himself wiggle room while answering the questions. He didn't want to lock himself into an answer that could have caused him some jeopardy. He was trying to answer the questions without directly lying. This is a common tactic that people in legal trouble will use to answer questions without specifically answering the question.

The purpose of parsing is to provide some cover later when another set of facts comes up that could be problematic for the person and they are called out about their previous answer. They can then respond that "Well that's not exactly what I meant, what I meant was, it depends on what is, is." This is an example of deception.

There are many examples of how words are used in a conversation to paint a picture one way or another, which means an investigator has to use active listening skills combined with an understanding of body language and how jeopardy affects a suspect to interpret the sometimes subtle clues of deception. That is what accomplished interviewers can learn to do over time, and it's what you want to achieve as well. Once we recognize the deception, we have to ask, why are they being deceptive? Is it to hide their guilt, shame, or embarrassment? This is how these skills guide the interviewer in their line of questioning.

The words we use mean things as much as the suspect's words. The suspect constantly looks for clues from the investigator about how much they know about him/her or the crime, how they feel about him, and whether they can successfully lie to the investigator. The clues the suspect is looking for are the words we use, and our body language so control of ourselves is vital to controlling the interaction with the suspect.

A QUICK QUESTION: DOES DECEPTION MEAN GUILT?

The quick answer is "no," deception on the part of a suspect does not mean they are guilty in terms of culpability for the crime or incident under investigation. What it can mean is that the person you are interviewing might have some knowledge of the incident or some other connection to the people involved in some way. They might be embarrassed that they hang around with the suspect, they might not want to get involved in the investigation for fear of "giving up" a friend, or divulging a bigger plot the suspect is involved in, or they may fear retaliation if they cooperate and talk to you.

When you see deception in a person you should call it out, be curious about it and pursue it. It may be nothing or it could be very important. You find out by recognizing deception, pursuing it, and asking the right questions.

Another good point to consider that goes along with our earlier talk about curiosity is that a question should almost always lead to another question. The more information we gather, the more questions we should be asking. Interviewers should habitually ask questions.

Next up, we're in the office with the suspect and ready to talk to them. In most cases, if it is a criminal interview and the reading of Miranda Rights is required, some investigators can become concerned that advising Miranda will cause the suspect to ask for an attorney, which is not always true. In fact, I have found that if you handle it correctly, most suspects will waive Miranda and move on. The following section talks a bit about this process.

Chapter 6 - The Miranda Warnings

FIRST IMPRESSIONS

First impressions are very important. The old saying that you get only one chance to make a first impression is absolutely true. There are some statistics that say people will look at another person and in the first minute of interaction decide what they think of them. In your private life, if that first impression is negative you may not make a friend, get a date, a job or a promotion.

If the first impression you give as a criminal investigator is negative, you may destroy any chance you have of building a bond and getting a confession.

Attention to this simple detail is therefore very important.

An effective tactic to take is to be professional and congenial to the person you are going to interview, no matter what you are investigating or what you suspect them of doing no matter how horrible the crime.

As we all know, advising a suspect, who is in custody, of their Miranda rights is fundamental to questioning a person suspected of committing a crime. We also know that the courts look very closely at how and when the Miranda rights were given and if the suspect fully understood their rights and then waived them in a knowing and voluntary way.

POLICE CUSTODY

What if the suspect is not in police custody?

The general rule of the advisement of Miranda rights is if you have custody of the person, they are not free to leave either on the street or in HQ, and you are going to question them about a crime they might be involved in they must be advised of their Miranda rights.

As per Lawinfo.com here is a good rule of thumb for advising Miranda rights.

When **Must** the Police Read Me My **Miranda Rights**? The **Miranda warning** is usually **given** when a person is arrested. However, the **Miranda Rights** attach during any "custodial interrogation" (when a person is substantially deprived of their freedom and not free to leave) even if the suspect hasn't been formally arrested. (Source: https://www.lawinfo.com/resources)

We should spend a few minutes covering this topic.

I also know that many investigators are concerned about the Miranda Rights Advisement. It would seem that telling someone they don't have to talk to you before you talk to them will lead to the majority of people invoking their Miranda rights and asking for an attorney before they speak to the police.

As I stated earlier, in reality it has been my experience that if you address the Miranda rights head on, in an open and clear way, the overwhelming majority of people will waive their rights and speak to you.

HERE'S MY THEORY ON MIRANDA WAIVER

Most of the people who are involved in criminal lifestyles become good liars; it's part of what they have to do to survive. They lie to their friends, their families, their victims and everyone else, which includes the police when need be. Because they lie all the time they think they can get over on us too.

And for people who are not full-time criminals, they believe that if they talk to us, they can convince us of their innocence and anyone who asks for a lawyer must be guilty, so they take their chance. A skilled interviewer can navigate Miranda without much trouble.

A few things to keep in mind when advising suspects of their Miranda rights:

1. **Some people will get upset when told you have to read them their rights.** That's OK. You can tell them it's your duty to do so to advise every one of their rights before discussing their case, or you can tell them that everyone interviewed in a police station gets their rights, it's part of what you do to protect them.

2. **Lots of people will ask you if they are under arrest because you read them their rights.** We all know that we advise many people that don't get arrested so unless they are actually under arrest at that moment you can tell them that being advised of their rights does not mean you are under arrest, but you can't get their side of the story if you don't tell them their rights and they agree to speak to you.

3. **Many people will tell you "I know my rights."** That's OK, but tell them you have to advise them anyway.

The second part of advising someone of their rights is that they must then give a knowing and voluntary waiver of those rights and agree to answer your questions.

This means they must understand their rights and then with that knowledge agree to talk to you. So spend a few minutes to get it right.

It's best to do the advisement on video and in writing so there is no question later how you made the advisement and that the suspect waived them. And if your video gets damaged you still have the written form.

As you read each right, ask them: "Do you understand that right?" and have them initial next to the line. This shows that they were aware of the right and signed off on it.

You should also end the reading by asking *"Do you understand each of the rights I have read to you? Do you have any questions about the rights I read to you? Will you speak to me now?"* If they do have questions, try to answer them.

Remember most interviews are now video or digitally re-corded. The judge, jury, lawyers and then the public will see how you handled this important part of the process. Do it right. Part of our job is to protect the rights of everyone, even the suspects.

To successfully get past the Miranda rights advisement and obtain a waiver from the suspect you must do a couple of things right away:

1. Be professional and not angry with the suspect.

2. Do not be accusatory from the start.

3. Do not portray that you are sickened by the person's actions.

4. Remain open to whatever they have to say and begin to build a bond with the subject.

5. Control your words and body language so they match your goals.

6. Really listen to the suspects answers.

7. Once they sign off on the Miranda form, put it away in an envelope or file, out of sight.

Chapter 7 -Interacting with Suspects, Victims and Witnesses

REALITY AND PROFESSIONALISM

Remaining professional and not revealing your true personal feelings about the subject or the crime they are suspected of is easy if you are investigating a theft, but the same is NOT true if you are investigating the sexual assault of a child or other horrible crime against a person. For most of us we would find ourselves disgusted by a person accused of such a crime and react to them accordingly in a negative way.

The professional investigator understands that you must go beyond your personal feelings if you are to properly investigate such a crime and obtain a confession.

Treating the person you are interviewing with disdain and contempt because of their actions will not help you build a bond with them, get them to trust you, or tell you want to know. You must understand this to be good at interviewing.

PRE-INTERVIEW CONVERSATIONS

Another important part of the interview process is the Pre-Interview conversation.

To call it a pre-interview is actually not a good description. As we all know, in most states in our country, the entire conversation between the law enforcement investigators and the suspect must be recorded on video or audio, so even this pre-interview conversation is actually part of your interview and will be recorded.

A term that more accurately describes this part of the process I will call the Pre-Crime Conversation part of the Interview. This is an important aspect of any interview. The Investigator must recognize the value in this part of your interaction with the suspect because it will help you build a bond with your subject and elicit the information you need to build a bond and obtain a confession. This is where we find "Possibilities" we can use in the interview!

When people come to a police station for any reason, most are nervous. When a person under suspicion of a crime comes to your police station they have even greater concerns. On top of being nervous they will also want to throw off any suspicion and get you to leave them alone. They will want to provide you with their alibi and leave as soon as possible.

The possibility of going to jail looms over their head and can complicate your ability to get the facts you seek.

Your job here is to:

1. Be professional.

2. Don't antagonize the suspect or otherwise cause them to be overly protective of every word they say.

3. Don't intimidate them by a show of authority.

4. Make them feel comfortable.

5. Give them confidence that they can speak freely.

6. Create an environment that does not say

    "You're going to jail" but instead says

    "We want to hear your side of things."

You can accomplish these goals by keeping in mind the things that the suspect fears and try to alleviate them as best you can. Remember what the perception of a police interview is like; people learn this from television. They often expect an overbearing cop to threaten them and force them to say things out of context. To trip them up and "catch them" in a lie.

If this is your style, you will not be successful. From my own experience I can tell you I have seen all kinds of interviewers including those TV-type guys that get in people's faces, tell them they better give it up or their going to jail or any other bullying tactic they can think of.

This style might work on an 18-year-old kid who has never been in trouble, but if you have to talk to someone who has been through the system and has been to jail before, the tough guy or tough girl approach is a waste of time.

Here is what works:

1. A calm demeanor.

2. Talk to the person respectfully.

3. Take the tactic that you are hoping they can help you clear up some parts of your investigation, that they might have information that can help the case and they might not even realize.

4. Offer them a drink (soda, water or juice).

5. Tell them you know they must feel nervous coming to a police station, but not to worry and to thank them for coming in.

Being rigid and acting like an authoritarian puts most people off—so be the opposite of that. These types of gestures go a long way to calming people down and when people are calm, they are easier to talk to.

The offering of food or drink comes up a lot in discussion about an interview with a suspect. Why do you care if they want a drink or something to eat? The answer here is simple: When the interview video is reviewed by a jury, lawyers, the judge and sometimes the public, how you treated the suspect will become a major issue. By offering a person a drink of water, a cup of coffee or something to eat (depending on the circumstances of course), you do two things:

First—When someone comes to your home, don't you usually offer them something to drink? It is part of what people do in a polite society and it helps begin the bond-building process.

Second—When the interview is reviewed, and you are seen having concern over the suspect's basic needs, you show compassion and everyone watching will see it. When and if the defendant later tries to say you were rude or overbearing, everyone watching the video will see you acting appropriately.

Never forget the cameras are running and it's your show.

LIGHTS, CAMERA, ACTION - IT'S YOUR SHOW - VIDEO/DIGITAL RECORDING OF INTERVIEWS

Almost every state requires video or digitally recording criminal statements for many crimes. This is actually a very good thing for the Investigator/Interviewer. and I think we should discuss this for a bit before moving on.

When I describe the video recording of a criminal statement as -"It's your show" I need you to understand that is not to take this lightly or treat it as a chance to make great movies. What I need you to understand is that in today's world people expect to see video or digital recordings of police interviews. In fact, what I have heard many people say is "if it isn't on video it didn't happen" or "the cops are lying". Understanding this is what should bring focus to your recorded interview.

It is your show means you should understand the power of video and the visual dynamics of your interview.

People will scrutinize every detail of the recoding to see where you were:

● Coercive

● Threatening

● Demeaning

● Violent

● Rude

● Inappropriate

● Mean

● Displaying bias against the suspect or witness

● Uncaring about the suspect or witnesses physical health or well being

When we understand this dynamic, we can make sure we address those issues in the recording to help prevent those kinds of lawyerly accusations later in the process.

Here are some suggestions to help you:

- Make sure you have a great recording system, one that perfectly syncs video with the audio, so the voice and picture are a perfect match. If it doesn't match up people will think it is doctored or faked or has been "adjusted" but law enforcement.

- Make sure the recording starts from the very first instant the suspect is brought into the interview room. In the best practices the recording should start before the suspect is brought into the room and continue until they are removed at the very end of the interview. If the interview goes on for 9 hours, even if the suspect or witness is taken to a rest room the room recording of the interview room should be on the whole time. Hallway cameras should show the suspect or witness going to the rest room and returning so on one can claim you had improper conversations when the suspect was out of the interview room.

- When you, the investigator / interviewer enter the room give the suspect a respectful and proper greeting.

- If they are injured in any way, ask about the injuries, and ask if they need anything. If they have cuts and bruises that have not been treated, ask about the injuries, and offer first aid right then and there. Have first aid respond to the interview room or have the first aid people treat then suspect in another location and ask them about the treatment when they return to the interview room. Show concern for the suspect. If they have a ripped "T: shirt or jeans, if they are muddy or wet ask if they want a clean shirt (Keep a supply of these in HQ).

- Consider offering them a cup of coffee, soda, or water and possibly food.

All of these things show you as a good and decent human being (They are also the right things to do for any other person) and demonstrate you were not overbearing or inappropriate with your suspect or witness. Remember, everyone see these recordings and they will all make a judgement about you and how you treated the suspect. Doing it right can save a lot of problems later in the process.

And they can remove negative comments or accusations from defense lawyers looking to create controversy over their client's statement, especially if it is a confession or admission. It will also demonstrate to the suspect/ witness that you have a concern for their well being, it helps a bond to build between you and the suspect.

Once you have set the proper tone, you don't want to jump right into your crime questions. If you pursue this avenue you're missing an opportunity to gather some valuable intelligence on your subject and find things to talk about later in the conversation when you are asking hard questions.

It is here in the Pre-Crime conversation area as you talk about non-threatening, non-crime topics you can learn a lot about your suspect.

For example, you can learn how to:

1. Gauge how a person answers questions.

2. See what they look like when they are answering truthfully to non-crime questions.

3. See how their body language looks when they are simply talking about non-important things like sports, jobs, and hobbies.

More on Setting a Baseline

As you gauge these baseline responses you are looking to see:

1. When they are just talking freely, do they look you in the eye?

2. Do they know the statistics for their favorite sports person's 2012 season at bats with great and immediate recall?

3. Do they laugh or act lighthearted when talking about their kids?

How people respond to non-crime questions will show you how they look and act when being truthful and relaxed without jeopardy. It also helps to put them at ease.

If you talk about their family you might hear about their sickly mother, their child on drugs, or their grandfather's war record. If you talk about life in general you might learn about their boss's nasty attitudes, their unemployment or marital status.

It is in this part of your non-crime question period that you can begin to develop a relationship with the subject. You find out who they are and where they are in life and get a feel from them and how they behave when there are no consequences on the table. All this information is priceless for the interviewer.

Remember an interview is a two-way street so you should engage with the subject. If they talk about work you can talk about what you did before you became a cop; you can talk about your life experiences.

Of course, we don't really want to discuss our family and friends with a suspect, but you should SOUND genuine when you discuss these things even if you are making them up.

A two-way nonthreatening conversation about mutual topics puts people at ease and helps establish a baseline for your conversation as well, because it brings people together and starts the development of a level of trust.

After all, wouldn't it be nice to know that someone is struggling to pay for the medical bills of their elderly parent if they are suspected of stealing a large amount of cash from their employer? Wouldn't that help you identify a motive and give you things to talk about with your suspect?

Of course, it would and that's why this pre-crime conversation time is extremely important and cannot be overlooked.

In case you're wondering, I might spend 10 to 20 minutes on this area before launching into the crime questions. I do whatever it takes for me to build a bond and get as many possibilities as I think I might need to overcome the denials and get a confession. So don't rush it, let them talk, value it.

As you transition from the Pre-crime Questions period to the Crime Questions, you should be aware of four (4) important factors.

The four things you need to do to move a subject toward a confession are discussed in the next chapter.

Chapter 8 - The Four Main Techniques, The Keys to the Kingdom

These are the main techniques when you put all the other parts of an interview, the concepts, the understanding of human emotions together, these are the four things you will use to move the interview forward.

This is where understanding that **Words Mean Things** comes into play. Using the previous descriptions, here is a more detailed explanation of the use of these techniques.

When we talk about the suspect's actions or the facts of the crime under investigation always remember to:

1. **Diminish** the description of the incident or crime.

2. **Rationalize** the person actions.

3. **Offer alternatives** for their actions.

4. **Display Compassion** to the person.

These four elements can make a difference in how the suspect perceives you and your intentions. They also help them view their perceived actions in a crime as more socially and morally acceptable, which can open the door to a conversation that builds a relationship leading to a confession.

Here's what I mean. Let's start with **diminishing the crime** description.

DIMINISHING

If you are investigating a car theft and you say, "The car was stolen" that is a hard description. To the suspect the word "stolen" represents a knowing violation of the law and is hard to confess to. It means they must say out loud that they are a thief, which can result in severe penalties.

A better alternative is to use a description like this:

"The car was taken." Taken is a much more relaxed way of expressing what happened, even though it means the same thing. Taken is a softer word than stolen; it doesn't convey the same immoral behavior.

It might seem like a minor difference but **WORDS MEAN THINGS**; diminishing the description of the crime by the words you use may allow the suspect to feel it is easier to take responsibility for their actions.

When Investigators are first exposed to this concept, they often feel that the simple choice of different words cannot really have that much effect; however, from experience, I can to you it makes a huge difference.

This is where understanding how people think helps you understand the concepts and how to use them effectively. Most people do not want to see themselves as being morally bad, even if they are bad and even if they do morally bad things.

The difference between doing these terrible things and admitting them out loud to another person is very difficult for people to do. Suspects will also associate a larger potential penalty with crimes the police see as "VERY SERIOUS" and therefore be less apt to admit to them.

Diminishing the description of the crime therefore makes the crime more acceptable and people are more likely to admit to it. If you really wanted to diminish the description of a car theft you could go even further and say something like:

"The car was borrowed without the owner's permission."

Think about those two descriptions "Stolen" or "Borrowed." Which one sounds less threatening to you?

Replacing the word stolen with borrowed may describe the same effect as far as the vehicle's owner is concerned; their car was taken, but how it sounds and feels to the suspect is much more acceptable. Everyone borrows things, bad people steal things.

When the suspect hears the investigator using these Diminished terms it makes them feel as though YOU don't see what they did as such a bad thing, therefore they will be more comfortable telling you they only meant to borrow the car.

Either way you still charge them with theft of the vehicle, but by diminishing the crime description you may also get a confession.

Other examples of diminishing the description of the crime with words we use in an investigation include:

1. "Raped," instead say—**"Had sex with"**

2. "Beaten or Assaulted," instead say—**"Hit"** or **"Slapped"**

3. "Burglarized," instead say—**"Went into the house"**

4. "Shot at," instead say—**"Fired the gun in the direction of"**

5. "Murdered or killed," instead say—**"Caused the death of"**

6. "Robbed," instead say—**"Took"**

The softening of these designations is all about perception. If the crime appeared to be less reprehensible to the police, then the suspect may feel less threatened by admitting their involvement.

I'm sure you get the idea.

I can't emphasize enough how important diminishing the description of the crime is. If you portray the suspect as a bad person and the crime is terrible or shocking, they will not want to admit to anything that is associated with those designations, and you will have difficulty obtaining a confession.

Diminishing Statements

You might use types of diminishing statements like this:

— *"I know you didn't mean to hurt anyone; you did something stupid,"* or

— *"Trying to feed your family is what we all do. By going to that gas station and taking the money from the clerk might have seemed like a way to solve your problem, but we both know it was a bad idea, wasn't it?"*

RATIONALIZING

After diminishing the description of the crime or incident the next step is to:

Rationalize the suspect's actions.

What does it mean to rationalize someone's actions in a criminal case investigation and interview? Is it the same as making a legal justification for their actions?

NO, it is a big difference.

Take, for example, a man protecting his home. An armed intruder enters his house and threatens to harm his family. He retrieves his gun and shoots the intruder killing him. This is still classified as a homicide, but it may be listed as Justifiable Homicide in the eyes of the court, because it was committed in the course of protecting his life and family.

The same is true for the police. If an officer has to use deadly force to protect herself or a third party and the suspect dies, it is still a homicide, but would ultimately be classified as a justifiable use of deadly force.

This concept of rationalizing is different in the interview process. What we mean is that we do not justify their actions in a legal sense. Instead, we give the suspect an alternative way to explain their actions that look more reasonable or face saving so they can admit to what they have done.

We do this by putting the best possible spin on whatever they have done, diminish the description of it and make it sound more acceptable. We help them rationalize it. Keep in mind this does not mean we agree with them or think what they did was right; it is categorized as a means to an end.

If the suspect believes we think they did something illegal for a plausible reason then they are much more likely to admit to doing it. The Investigator has significant power over the suspect if he/she has carefully built a bond and allowed a trust to develop.

We want to foster the idea in the mind of the suspect that they cannot lie their way out of the situation and that YOU, the investigator, are their best hope for getting the best deal possible for their actions. This forces them to see you as an ally and not so much as an adversary.

Let's take this example:

During a drug deal at an apartment an argument over the price arises and a fight breaks out. The suspect pulls a gun and purposefully shoots and kills the dealer, then steals the drugs and the money. This is a classic murder during a narcotics deal.

You have to interview the suspect. If you start off by accusing him of murder and taking a tough stance against him, he will get the very clear message that anything he says to you will put him in jail for a long time, if not get him a death sentence. There is not much chance of getting a confession here.

But ... perhaps you decided to take a different stance and use the diminishing technique and rationalize their actions. You could start your interview by telling the suspect that you knew how bad the drug dealer was and that you knew he had been convicted in the past for aggravated assault. It was your investigative theory that the drug dealer attacked the suspect and the suspect had to defend himself, which lead to the killing, and it is your job to get the suspect's side of the story for the record.

This mollifying approach places you, the investigator, in a totally different light and starts the relationship off on a totally different basis. The suspect may see you as gullible or even stupid; but if they believe they can convince you that they were acting in self-defense, what better ally could they have than an investigating cop on their side?

Although this scenario is abstract, it is not uncommon. The same principles that work in a homicide case work in a shoplifting case and everything in between because you are dealing with human beings.

The level of the problem and the penalties they face is certainly different, but the reality that the person is in trouble is the same, which creates jeopardy for them. Their goal is to alleviate their jeopardy, and to get out from under the burden of punishment for their actions. If they can convince you they are innocent or their actions were somehow justified, they have a chance; so let them tell you their side of the story. Let them talk.

This is like a game, a mental game:

They have reasons to lie and avoid detection. You, on the other hand, have an obligation to overcome the obstacles to attain the truth and get them to admit their guilt.

This result is achieved by understanding how people think and using tactics to overcome their resistance.

So, by taking this diminished description of the incident, the suspect may very well start talking to you, and give you details of the incident you may not otherwise have known.

To be sure they will most likely give you details and information that back up their story and show they were not in the wrong. Early on that's OK, because it allows you to build a bond and get them talking.

OUR First goal in any interview:

Is to get the suspect to put themselves at the scene and committing the action regardless of why they say they did it or how it happened. In this scenario, we need the suspect to tell us they were in the apartment buying drugs and shooting the dealer.

As the investigation continues, and you and the suspect fill in the details, you can begin to take apart the suspects story using crime scene evidence, other interview skills, forensic evidence, or other witnesses.

However, once they say they were at the scene, shooting the victim, they can't go back and say they were never there, or they didn't pull the trigger. All they can do is begin altering their story to fit the evidence.

If you are smart and play along, you will gather more information to use later on in the interview or interrogation phase to destroy the lies and prove their guilt.

Once their story starts to come apart and they see the reality of your investigation and where it's leading, then jeopardy will return. They will look for a lifeline. If you have built a bond with them you will be that lifeline. You can then help them accept their actions.

You can then tear apart the lies, and with each exposed layer you get closer to the truth.

As you move through the process, as long as you are still talking, you can introduce evidence that reveals their story to be a lie. This will move you closer to the truth.

As you refute their lies, they will have to confront the facts, which will change the tone of the conversation. People will often show you that they know their story is falling apart and the truth is becoming clearer. They may show this more by physical gestures than words (Body Language); they may show you they know they cannot get away with the crime by slouching their shoulders, breathing deeply, or looking off into the distance as if help were on the horizon.

Laying off or rationalizing their actions on things like:

1. It was a stupid thing to do.

2. It seemed like a good idea at the time.

3. It was a dumb thing to do.

4. A lot of people would have done the same thing.

5. You never thought all this would happen.

6. Your intention wasn't for this thing to go this far, was it?

7. You didn't start out the day saying, "I'm going to get involved in this," did you?

8. If you could take it back you would, wouldn't you?

These kinds of comments can go a long way to winning over the suspect. You have to get comfortable using them. You can do that by practicing all the time on any one you have a conflict with. In time they will become second nature and you will become a very proficient interviewer.

OFFER ALTERNATIVES

Offer alternatives for their actions—This technique falls under the possibility's category. By offering more acceptable reasoning for their crimes, you can help the suspect accept their action, especially if they think you don't find them to be a horrible person.

Offering alternatives, like saying you think they acted in self-defense or they were just trying to feed their kids can sound very inviting to a person in serious trouble, so much so they may realize they are not leaving the station but if they go with the alternatives you offer they may get leniency from the court or have other options.

Similar to exchanging harsh words for softer words when diminishing their conduct, offering alternatives helps the suspect to involve themselves in the situation under more socially acceptable circumstances.

This brings us to the last step in the process, the thing that may take them over the finish line and get them to confess the truth:

DISPLAYING COMPASSION

The use of compassion is another acknowledgment that we are dealing with human beings. There comes a time in every investigation when the suspect may see the futility of continuing to lie.

They may see you as their lifeline to the best deal they are going to get, they may accept that they will have to pay a penalty for their actions, but they will still resist providing a truthful confession. They may very well be afraid of the consequences that await them, and they stall, freeze and cannot go further.

This is where **Compassion** can be the best tool in your toolbox.

Compassion is a powerful emotion. When a person feels alone, when they feel the fear of what is to come, there is often a confusion that over takes the mind.

Having someone they trust and have a relationship with, even a short-term relationship like that of the suspect and interviewer, can work to your advantage.

By understanding what the suspect is feeling you can reach out to them with compassion. You can tell them you know how hard it's going to be for them and their family when the truth comes out. You can tell them you know they are afraid to say what they did because of the fear of jail.

But you can also tell them that you have gotten to know them and understand why they did what they did, even if it was wrong. You can tell them that at this point the best thing they can do is be honest, show remorse for their actions and ask everyone in the system to recognize they know what they did was wrong.

Tell them how the system works, we have all seen the TV news and court TV shows where the whole world is waiting for the guilty person to be "Sorry" for what they did and how most people are willing to show some form of forgiveness for those who accept responsibility and express their remorse.

You tell them that you will tell the court that they expressed sorrow and told the truth and that their actions were not intended to cause such pain. You will be their ally.

This may all be untrue on your part. You may find the suspect to be a disgusting example of a human being, deserving of life in prison but, until you get the confession with the truth, you have to keep working the interview and building a bond.

The display of Compassion combined with their sense of being alone, can be the exact recipe to break the final wall of resistance.

When we are new at this type of work these concepts seem improbable at best and a waste of time at worst, but I can tell, as can any good interviewer, that if you use them and get good at them they work very well.

In the course of my career I have been shocked at the response by suspects that have been charged with the most horrible crimes. I have worked them, using the techniques I described, I have been patient and when it was over I have had many of them thank me. I even had one man hug me and thank me for getting him through the process. That was life changing for me and revealed very clearly that these concepts and tactics do work and they are very, very powerful ...

BUILDING A BOND

I have talked about the need to build a bond with the people you interview if you expect that they will confess to you. The logical question is: *How do you do that? How do you develop and bond with a killer, a drug dealer or a thief?*

Many of the people we deal with as investigators are truly horrid people. They have done terrible things to their victims that shock our consciousness and often sicken us.

That being said we have to get beyond those feelings. We have to find it in ourselves to see the higher goal and do the things necessary to accomplish our mission and bring justice for our victims.

We can do this by getting the correct mindset. That mindset is very similar to the mindset you need to conduct undercover operations. In an undercover operation you have to become someone else, you have to pretend and really immerse yourself in the part if you are to be successful. Same thing here.

You have to see the suspect as a resource. They have something you need and you have to immerse yourself in their world to get it. You must put aside your personal feelings about the person or their crime and you may have to pretend.

You might have to pretend to like them; pretend to care about them, pretend to understand them and be willing to get close to them physically and emotionally if you are to succeed.

Some investigators can't do this. Some investigators have a very hard time not only understanding the concept, but finding it impossible to sit in a room with a killer and treat them well; that is, to laugh with them and to listen to their twisted logic or tortured version of the truth.

That's OK. Not everyone is suited for this type of work. But I can tell you from experience, if you want to do good in your career, if you want to feel a sense of satisfaction, then getting a hardened criminal to admit their crimes is one of the most intense things you can experience as a law enforcement professional, but only you know where you fit in. If you want to do this work you can become good at it and make a difference.

The answer to the question: How do you build a bond with the suspect? lies in your belief in the mission you are on—to obtain a confession from a person who has committed a crime, no matter what that crime is. You do it because it is what's needed to be done to accomplish your mission. Simple.

The four techniques described earlier: Diminish the Crime Description, Rationalize the Suspect's Actions, Offer Alternatives and Display Compassion are tried and true methods of creating an environment where someone will talk to you. Practice them and use them.

Chapter 9 - Human Reactions

PHYSICAL SIGNALS TO LOOK FOR DURING AN INTERVIEW

There are some breathing signals we can look for as well. When a human being is confronted with a dangerous situation they can fall into the "Fight or Flight" mentality. This means when there is danger afoot, a person will prepare to protect themselves by preparing to fight the danger or take flight to run from the danger.

One of the ways our bodies prepare us for this fight or flight is to take a deep breath to fill our system with oxygen. I call this and "Fortifying" breath as we are preparing to engage the danger.

In an interview you might see a fortifying breath taken by the suspect or witness right after you ask a serious question about their actions in an incident or crime. They take the breath to get ready to fight you off verbally and mentally. You might see them draw in a big breath and hold it for a second, then begin their lying.

The next kind of breath signal we can see in an interview is a "Cleansing" breath. A cleansing breath is taken by a suspect usually when they are defeated and ready to confess or make admissions. Remember the mind and body are connected. Just as the fortifying breath is taken before a fight, a cleansing breath is taken by a person just before they give up the information or confess. You might see them take a deep breath hold it, then exhale very deeply to the point they are emptied out of air physical and mentally. They may slump down as they exhale as the resistance is gone from them, they are cleansed and ready to reveal information.

These are good physical signs to look for and come under the body language arena.

A CASE STUDY / SEX OFFENDER INTERVIEW

In the following description of an interview I conducted with a man who was serving 6 years for the sexual assault of two 12-year-old boys you will see how the use of the techniques of bonding and compassion were used to elicit the confession. This was a very difficult interview to conduct for three reasons, One the man was in year 5 and half of his 6-year sentence and he was preparing for release from prison. Reason Two, I had to conduct the interview in the prison and Three, I had arrested him for drunk driving several years earlier.

Making a connection to this person was difficult because we had a history, the drunk driving arrest, and also because of the nature of his crimes and his personal sexual predatory activities towards children, which I found reprehensible.

Regardless, of all those factors my duty was to conduct my investigation and interview him and attempt to get his to confess to a new crime, one that involved children and that he committed while in prison!

Case Study

A Sex Offender in Prison, a Letter and Nude Pictures of Children

This case started when a woman about 35 years old walked into HQ and asked to speak to a detective. I met with her and she was visibly nervous. She told me her longtime boyfriend was in state prison for molesting 2 twelve-year-old boys. When he got caught, he admitted to the crime and took a 6-year prison sentence as a first-time offender.

His six years was up in another 5 months and he mailed her an envelope in advance of his release. Her hand shaking, she gave me the envelope. I opened it. Inside was a letter from her boyfriend telling her he was coming home soon and asking her to hold onto some pictures for him that he described as "Important."

I looked at the pictures and they were commercial photos of young children about the ages of 3 and 4. The kids were naked. The woman had a 13-year-old daughter and she was confused and afraid about what this man would do when he got home from jail; would he attack her daughter?

She wanted to know where he got the pictures of naked kids while he was in jail for molesting kids! Reasonable questions to be sure. As any of us that have worked in law enforcement and corrections know, anything can and does end up in our jails.

I investigated her complaint; the crimes were considered harassment under Domestic Violence laws because she was annoyed and alarmed at the content of the letter. A bigger question was the pictures of the naked children.

When I asked officers what crime was committed by sending those pictures, they almost all say, "distributing kiddie porn." But is it?

Does the possession and sending of pictures of naked children constitute kiddie porn? I usually ask the officers if their parents had pictures of them as little children and they were naked? They almost always say yes. I then ask if mom is a pornographer? NO, of course not they say. So, what makes it kiddie porn?

In most jurisdictions any photo or drawing of a child engaged in any kind of sex act is kiddie porn, but a photo of a naked child is not considered so unless it is used for the sexual gratification of any person. That means if someone looks at a photo of a naked child and objectifies that child sexually, then it can be considered kiddie porn.

I was going to move forward on this investigation, but I knew that the man that sent the photos would have to admit to using the photos for sexual gratification to charge him with anything substantial. This meant I had to go to the jail and interview him 5 months before his release date and get him to admit how he used the pictures. It seemed like a tough job, and it was.

My boss said it wouldn't work, even my partner said it wouldn't work, but I had to try, it was my job and, besides, I was curious about this guy and this crime and wanted to know if I could get him to confess.

I made arrangements to meet him in the jail and interview him. I had an investigator from the jail with me, but he didn't think I would have much luck either.

The suspect came into the room in his brown jail overalls and sat down. It was at that moment I realized I had arrested him early in my career for DWI, drunk driving. Obviously, this can be a problem because he could harbor negative feelings about me that could ruin the interview. There was also the possibility that he wouldn't remember me at all. I had to make a decision—bring up the DWI arrest or take my chances on a faulty memory.

I believed the best course of action was to deal with the problem head on and clear it up in the beginning. If he could not deal with me the interview would be over right away, if he could get past it, I had a better chance of talking to him.

I immediately brought up the DWI arrest by asking him "Hey, don't I know you?"

He looked at me and said, "Yeah you arrested me for drunk driving."

I had to think quick. Remember that most people are self-centered, or "me centered" as I call it, meaning they care about themselves first and foremost. Knowing this I asked—"You didn't end up as an alcoholic and hurting yourself or anything did you?" By asking this I was showing concern for him first.

He thought about it and said "No, I was just drinking too much that day.... What do you want now?" The gamble paid off, but it reveals we should always address any conflicts up front and clear the air.

At this point I had no idea how to proceed, how do you bring up the topic at hand. Do you just explain it factually and ask if he is committing crimes with the pictures?

I was dancing no doubt and wasn't sure where to go. The reality here is that the man had a sexual deviancy. Sex is a base drive in humans, it is one of the things we can struggle to control if we have a tendency to allow our sex drive to push us to crime as this man's did. The sex drive and the things that motivate us sexually are individual in each person and that is why sexual criminals rarely "get better." They usually learn how to suppress it so they can be released, but their sex drive doesn't change.

I knew I had to connect to this man's disposition, but how? I am not attracted to young children and pretending I was to get him to talk would not work, he would recognize the lie and the lack of genuineness, which would leave me with no credibility.

So, I turned to a different way to get into his head. I came up with this story, and although it was a fabrication, it was within my zone and I could pull it off.

"You know my wife is a blonde and I love my wife."

That was my opening line. The man stared at me like I had just fallen out of the sky. I imagine he had no idea why I would say that, but I kept going.

"I love my wife more than anything in the world, but you know what makes me crazy, I mean really crazy?"

He looked at me, and I could see he was intrigued.

"Redheads. Redheads make me nuts! I don't know what it is about them, but when I see a redhead, I can't stop looking, like I'm drawn to them and can't control it. So last week I'm out to dinner with my wife, we're talking at the table and a redhead comes into the restaurant. She catches my eye and I can't stop staring at her. I followed her across the room with my eyes. My wife saw this and shoved me saying I was a jerk. I apologized and tried to control myself, but it was hard to do. I kept looking around the room for the redhead, sneaking glances here and there to find her."

As I was telling him this, I moved my chair closer to him and continued.

"No matter how hard I tried I couldn't stop looking for the redhead, then I saw her, and my heart skipped a beat, you know what I mean?"

At this point he was listening to my story intently, it caught his attention and connected to him. He looked at me and said, "Yes, I know what you mean."

I moved even closer to him and asked him if that was why he sent the pictures to his wife, if that was why they were important to him?

He looked around the room at the jail investigator then back at me. I moved right next to him and said "Listen, it's just you and me here, two men being honest, what do you do with the pictures? Do you masturbate looking at them?"

This is an awkward place to be in, but I wanted the confession, a few minutes of my discomfort was worth the effort to keep a pedophile in jail.

The man leaned into me and I saw a bead of sweat running down the side of his head. It felt like a breakthrough. He looked down at the floor, then back at me. I could see he was thinking, trying to figure out what to do. I could sense his isolation. It was here that I reached out and touched his shoulder to let him know I was with him. I saw the reaction he was jolted by the touch and his head twitched. I looked at him without saying a word I just nodded. He looked down at the floor again and said—"Yes, I do, I'm all alone in here, and I can't help it."

What he didn't say was "Like you can't help looking at redheads." We had connected and he gave me what I needed because I worked for it. After his admission I calmly asked him if he would give me a typed statement, just to clarify what we talked about.

When I said that it was like he came out of a trance, he sat up, his eyes cleared and he said—"That's a second-degree crime, I won't put that in writing." That statement told me that he was well aware of what he was doing, he knew it was wrong. Unfortunately for him I had a witness to his confession, and I charged him. He got an additional 6 months jail time for his admission, less than I hoped, but he was held to account.

The main points of this story are this:

1. Even an interview that seems impossible can be done if we try and use our skills.

2. Developing things to talk about in the interview requires quick thinking sometime.

3. Understanding human nature and how to connect can be very powerful.

I left that jail more confident than ever that I could be an excellent interviewer. That incident shows that if you understand what makes people tick and how they think and you use the correct approach, skills, and control your own emotions, you can overcome the most difficult of odds.

Truth be told, I was disgusted by this man and what he did. After he made the admissions, I felt like I needed to shower, but I did my job. I got the confession and that is our goal as Investigators.

As hard as it was, I built a bond with the man in the jail interview. I allowed myself to enter his world; I had to convince him that I understood what he was doing, and because I could understand it, and he believed I did something similar myself, he felt bonded to me and could then admit what he did. I helped him rationalize his actions and I was willing to enter his world.

If you spend your time telling people only how terrible they are and how disgusting their thoughts and actions are, it will prevent you from establishing a trust with them, and they will not confess.

Chapter 10 - Interview Preparation

PERSONAL INVENTORY

A good interviewer has to prepare before any interview, which means doing research before you sit down with the subject.

Here are some ways to prepare yourself for the interview:

1. Know the facts of your case inside and out.

2. Do a thorough background on every person you interview.

3. Read other statements from other involved people.

4. Review any available crime scene photos or evidence so you know the layout of the place where the incident took place.

5. Learn about your victim(s), their life, lifestyle, friends, habits, work and family.

Preparation will put you in a good place to engage in the conversation.

The final step is mental. Be prepared to go the distance. Some interviews can last for hours.

THE UNDERSTANDING AND USE OF POSSIBILITIES

Possibilities are what we call a series of potential excuses that you, the interviewer, covertly suggest to the suspect during the interview process to explain their actions during an incident.

The purpose of these Possibilities is to encourage the suspect to admit involvement in a crime or incident for reasons other than the truthful reasons they committed the act. You give them more acceptable motives they can admit to.

As an example: if a woman kills her husband for insurance money, it is reasonable to assume that she knows this is murder for profit and she will be treated very severely in the court system. It is also a good bet she will not just simply confess to her crime and tell you the terrible truth of why she killed him; however, a skilled interviewer knows this reality and will offer some alternative possibilities to the suspect to explain her actions so that she can mitigate her real criminal behavior.

What I might say to this suspect is something like this:

"I know that in many marriages there are hidden things that go on behind closed doors. Not every husband is a great guy, some husbands can be outwardly wonderful but brutal when no one is looking. Did you and your husband have any problems like that?"

This Possibility is obvious. I am asking the suspect to jump on the "Yes he hit me, and I was just protecting myself" band wagon. She might see this as a reasonable excuse for shooting her husband, accept it, and then fabricate her story to match that reasonable and acceptable possibility.

In the suspect's mind the possibility provides her with some cover for her actions, cover that may not look like criminal behavior. Possibilities go right along with diminishing—they work hand in hand.

Possibilities then are alternative motives the suspect can latch onto to explain their criminal behavior in a way that sounds more acceptable and plausible so they can explain their behavior and avoid responsibility and punishment.

Remember, during the initial part of our interview, we don't care why they put themselves at the scene of the crime committing an illegal action, the goal is to get them to admit being there and doing something. Further conversation between you and the suspect will bring out the truth. Even if they refuse to tell you anything but their concocted story, your investigation, along with the physical evidence and other statements will prove what actually happened.

Remember this: No matter how convoluted, strange or unusual the truth of an event is, if you tell it as a truth, it doesn't

change. A lie on the other hand can and does change— often as new facts are added. In a criminal interview the suspect's story should not change when new facts are presented, if it does, that is a sign of deception.

WHY DO THEY LIE?

So why don't people just realize they are caught and tell the truth?

Most suspects you interview will be very reluctant to just come out and admit their guilt.

There are many reasons for this, such as:

1. Fear of punishment (jail or worse)

2. Loss of financial opportunities

3. Humiliation (friends and family finding out)

4. Arrogance (cops won't be able to figure it out)

When you look at this list it covers just about every reason someone would be reluctant to tell you the truth. A good interview will overcome these concerns and the truth will be revealed.

SO WHERE DO WE GET THE POSSIBILITIES?

We get the possibilities from the suspect themselves, from the things they tell us in the pre-interview conversations before any crime questions are asked.

If you listened to the suspect during this pre-interview and you guided the conversation from his/her—family/job/lifestyle/ hobbies/health and other personal conversational topics you will have heard many things you can look to for Possible excuses the person might feel comfortable with.

Possibilities, therefore, represent all of the things that the person you are interviewing might feel are reasonable excuses for why they did what they did.

We use Possibilities as a device to find out what those potentially acceptable excuses are, so we can build a bond to the person and help them accept their responsibility in a way that does not make them have to admit they are bad and to lessen or remove the potential punishment for their action. A relief of their jeopardy.

HERE'S HOW IT WORKS—DIMINISHING THE DESCRIPTION OF THE CRIME.

A person who steals alcohol because they want to go to a party with an expensive bottle of booze to impress everyone is not in the same category as a man who steals bread to feed his starving children. Though both acts are illegal, isn't one of them much more acceptable in society's eyes than the other?

Wouldn't we all have sympathy for someone trying to feed their children?

In fact, if your kids were hungry and you had no money, would you consider stealing to feed them?

If we are honest with ourselves, I believe we would have to say yes, we would do whatever we needed to do to take care of our families. This concept, of stealing to feed your starving kids, is a possibility that we throw out to the suspect to explain their actions. If they were stealing bread to sell to buy drugs, they might not want to admit to that, but stealing to feed their kids is considered much more acceptable; therefore, they might latch onto that excuse, that possibility, and admit what they had done.

So, if I were interviewing someone for stealing bread, I wouldn't accuse them of "stealing bread," I might ask them— *"Were you taking that bread for anyone else? Do you have a family or kids you're trying to feed?"*

To a suspect this approach might seem quite acceptable. After all, who can argue with trying to feed your kids? It can even be seen in some places as an honorable thing to do, even though illegal.

And for us, we, at this point in the process, don't care if they really are stealing bread to feed their kids. Our first goal is to get them to admit stealing the bread. If we use this rationalization as a means of admission, we win. We can flesh out the details and get to their real motivations once we get beyond the responsibility barrier and they admit they took the bread.

To better understand this rationalization concept, we have to ask if it has any place in our lives already.

RATIONALIZING ACTIONS

To answer that, let's look at our larger society, isn't there a huge movement to tax the rich and take what some people consider their extra money for the good of those who have less. And indeed aren't the rich of our society often portrayed as bad and evil. In many minds taking from them is honorable and the right thing to do. Rob from the rich to give to the poor is an adage we all know from childhood.

It's the same concept of rationalizing an action, and it works.

In other criminal cases you would do the same thing; look for some acceptable possibilities as to why the suspect committed the crime, such as:

1. **Committing a robbery**—To get money for a sick mother's medicine, pay for a sick child's doctor, get food for a family member or friend or yourself.

2. **Committing a sexual assault**—He/She came on to you, he/she told you she/he was 18, he/she said she/ he wanted to be with you, she/he wanted you to teach him/her how to have sex.

3. **Committing murder**—They attacked you first, you thought they had a gun; you were protecting someone else; you never intended to kill anyone, you just wanted them to stop.

4. **Selling drugs**—To make money to pay the rent, feed the kids and get to rehab.

5. **Burglary**—You need stuff and you didn't think anyone would be home, people have insurance and they could get reimbursed, you were high or drunk, you thought it was a friend's house.

6. **Theft**—You intended to pay it back, it was just a loan, and you needed it to pay for medicine.

The list goes on and on, but the same basic concept runs through all of these examples. Whatever the person did, you need to look for a socially acceptable excuse for their actions, or a way to play off their involvement. Some people call this blaming the victim, especially in sex-assault cases.

In reality we know we are not blaming the victim, but we cannot confuse our sympathetic feelings for an innocent victim and our goal of getting a guilty suspect to admit to their actions. If you have to play along with the suspect's perceptions or story line to gain their confidence and build a bond that can lead to them confessing, then you have to do it.

Political correctness has no place in a police investigation. We cannot avoid doing and saying things that will help us solve the crime simply because some people not involved with the investigation might find our tactics offensive. So if you have to accept the suspect's version of what took place to get them to talk, then you do that.

It doesn't feel or sound nice, but your first goal as the investigator is to establish several very important things, specifically:

1. What was done

2. Who was involved

3. How it happened

4. Why it happened

The more serious the crime involved, the more your suspect will deny culpability or involvement. If you do not overcome these basic obstacles then you cannot be successful.

To make a successful prosecution we must establish that the suspect did something criminal, to a person or thing, how the action took place and why they did it.

THE INVESTIGATOR MUST UNDERSTAND HUMAN NATURE

When confronted about their involvement in a crime most people will do one or more of these things:

1. Deny any involvement.

2. Diminish their involvement.

3. Provide only partial information, leaving out the information that reveals their criminal actions.

4. Blame others for the incident.

5. Invoke self-defense.

6. Blame drugs or alcohol.

7. Feign forgetfulness or lack of a memory.

8. Provide faulty information meant to mislead the investigation or provide an alibi for themselves.

9. Accuse the investigator of inappropriate motives for the investigation or suspicion upon them.

10. Blame a set up for any facts that point to them.

You may get some or all of these thrown at you by the suspect. You must maintain your professionalism and use your skills to overcome these obstacles.

FIRST OBSTACLE

Our priority is to get the person to put themselves at the scene of the crime.

It doesn't matter what they initially tell us was the reason they were there, we have to get them to admit they were there.

Next, we have to get them to implicate themselves in the criminal actions. Again, we don't care why or how they say they became involved, the key is to link them to the criminal actions. How did it happen? This is the M.O. or Modus Operandi. What were the mechanics of the criminal action? After getting them to put themselves at the scene of the crime and engaging in actions of the crime, we would then like to know why they did it.

WHY?

The "why" of a criminal act can be the most difficult thing to find out from your suspect.

The suspect may tell you what happened; for example, they broke into a house to steal property from the owner. They may tell you they did this by kicking in the back door to gain entry to the house and stole clothing because their kids needed it. If that is all you have, a simple theft of clothing, the why might be simple too. They had no money and needed clothes.

But if your crime is a more complicated situation, say a burglary and sexual assault of an adult child in the house, you may get the suspect to tell you how they got into the house and you might get them to admit they had sex with the victim (especially if you have physical evidence), but when it comes to the why of a crime like this you may never get the real truth from your suspect. The reason being: they can make acceptable excuses for committing the burglary but making a reasonable excuse for having sex with a child is impossible.

If they were truthful, they might have to say OUT LOUD that they are sexually attracted to prepubescent boys or girls and the idea of having sex with a 3- or 4-year-old is the greatest sexual thrill they can imagine. Saying this truth out loud carries with it so much societal condemnation that the average sexual pervert will protect this truth at all costs, sometimes even from themselves.

In a case like this, or with any morally perverse crime, you may have to settle for the excuses they give to your possibilities and allow the jury to weigh their reasons. It is up to the investigator to be aware of the crime they are dealing with and the suspect's background and mental state when determining how far to push for the why of a crime.

Just as in my story of the man in jail revealed, he knew what he was doing was not only illegal, but it was morally objectionable as well. He would not openly reveal his attraction to underage children honestly, even though I managed to get him to reveal his sexual attraction to them to me in the bubble we created during the interview as we bonded.

The same is true for many serial killers. They can tell you the how of their crimes, but the why is often a vague, nonsensical rambling. Because to state the truth, that they are a sexual deviant that finds torturing and killing of a helpless victim and the use of them as a sex slave with no regard for their victim's humanity overpowering, is something even people involved in these crimes cannot admit out loud.

Instead, they will provide a litany of more acceptable reasons for their actions such as the victim wanted rough sex and it got out of hand, or the victim hurt them in some way during the sex and they reacted and injured the victim, or they accidentally killed the victim and then panicked and hid the body.

In the mind of the criminal:

These types of excuses are examples of the suspect trying to diminish their culpability in a crime. If they can't avoid being identified as being involved then the next thing to do is diminish their involvement or create a plausible reason for their actions.

THE STAGES OF AN INTERVIEW

Most interviews that end up being successful have definite stages, such as:

1. Denial of involvement—it wasn't me or I wasn't there.

2. I was there but I didn't do it.

3. I did it, but I had good reason.

4. The truth.

Using your skill and select pieces of evidence to destroy their lies will usually be the thing that moves the interview from one phase to the next, but not always. That's where the interrogation phase can sometimes be the answer. We will discuss that next.

Your job as the investigator is to understand the stages the interview will usually take, then recognize each stage as it unfolds and use the right technique to move the suspect to the next stage.

As you go along you will peel apart their story layer by layer until it becomes clear to you and the suspect that further lying is useless. Even if you reach this point the suspect may still hold on and refuse to admit their guilt.

Knowing that the interview is a back-and-forth process where you discuss the situation and try to guide the suspect to a confession using skill and facts, you may have to move on to a stronger tool: the Interrogation.

UNDERSTANDING INTERROGATION

As per our initial definitions, an interview is a conversation between two people and an Interrogation is an assertive, one-sided statement of the investigators determination of what happened and why. It is directly accusatory.

Being assertive does not mean being threatening to the suspect. It really means being persistent in your version of the truth and pressing forward.

If we threaten a suspect we jeopardize our entire case. Even if we don't mean to be threatening, but the suspect interprets your action as threatening, the defense attorney will portray even the slightest hint of a threat as coercion and use that to get the jury to believe the suspect only confessed out of fear of you.

Besides that reality, there is the responsibility we have as law enforcement people. We want the truth to come from fact, not from fear. We should never intimidate anyone to get a confession, and we don't have to.

Conducting a great interview or Interrogation will get you what you need without fear or intimidation.

Here's how we transition to an Interrogation:

You realize the interview phase is over when the suspect looks like they are ready to give in, but they don't. When you have no new areas to explore and you need to increase the intensity to overcome their defiance or adherence to their lies, you should tell them that you feel you both need a break. Tell the suspect you are going to leave for a minute and you will be back after you get some additional information.

Ask if they want a drink or need to use the bathroom and take care of those needs.

Then leave them in the interview room alone.

Take about 3 to 4 minutes before you go back in. When you return to the room your demeanor should be more rigid and determined. The time for talking is over.

Enter seriously, when you return. Your partner should sit quietly.

During the interrogation we do not allow the suspect to interrupt us or change the interrogation flow. Stop them cold if they try make any more denials.

Interrogation is the subject of another book, but I want to at least give you a minute on the topic and where it might fit into the overall scheme of your investigation.

The subject may have several reactions to this new phase of the investigation and your actions:

1.   They may realize you will not listen to any more lies and they will shake their heads yes or say they did it.

2.   They may look shocked (fake) and shake their head NO and mouth "I didn't take anything."

3.   They may answer very forcefully that they didn't do it.

No matter what they say, other than to admit their guilt, you must stop them from lying any further.

Some suspects may make a confession at this point, others may engage in more interview-like conversation and offer up some additional information that they held back earlier. You may choose to return to an interview footing if you feel truthful information is coming out and the suspect is now willing to talk. You can transition back and forth in some cases you will have to decide on a case-by-case basis.

It's hard to say how many times you may have to do this, but rely on your experience and see how it's working. If the suspect looks like their weakening, but still not confessing, you might want to switch gears and use the relationship you've built. Try throwing out some Possibilities and be compassionate.

"Push Lines"

A push line is used when the suspect is on the verge of confessing. All the signs are there they just need a little more encouragement. A push line is designed to nudge the suspect into confessing by linking the criminal action to an innocuous, non-dangerous and societally understandable motive, which will often result in the suspect telling you the truth.

Some push lines can include:

1. You made a mistake, you didn't intend to commit a crime.

2. You did something stupid, you weren't thinking.

3. You never intended to hurt anyone, it was an accident.

4. You're not that kind of person everyone I've talked to has said that would commit this action, it just happened right?

These push lines are specifically created to limit a person's belief in their culpability. If you see their will is fading and they are responding, you can use these push lines to create that final belief that you understand them and see their actions as less than evil.

Saying something like this might work:

"Bob, listen, I know you're afraid to tell me you took the money, but I'm telling you a jury is going to see the truth that my investigation shows, and they are going to convict you. I spent all day with you and it's clear to me you did this, it will also be clear to everyone else that you did it. Wouldn't it be better to be a man and take responsibility for your actions and tell the truth, and admit you did something really stupid rather than to have them think you are just some dirtbag thief?"

Wait for the response. Then move ahead with a further question and response or more Push Lines. Either way keep at it, going back and forth until you get where you want to be. In many cases, where you a good relationship with the subject or have actual evidence, the subject will confess at this point. The more serious the crime, the more likely they are to confess.

Human nature tells us that a very serious crime places a terrible mental burden on people. Most people want to tell the truth but resist to avoid the consequences. Once that's eliminated, they very often want to relieve that mental burden and get it off their chests by confessing. That's why we keep pushing.

We interview first then transition into an interrogation if necessary. That's the right path, we should never start with an interrogation-type conversation and think we can go backward, that does not work. Stick to the right path. Try to talk it out of them first, then interrogate if you have to.

OTHER THINGS TO LOOK FOR

Now that we have an understanding of some very important concepts, ideas and skills about interviewing and interrogating let's take a few minutes to touch on some other topics related to human nature and people's behavior so you will recognize some of the signs people give with their **nonverbal communication.**

Human beings are unique individual creatures that share some common traits. These traits are based on the fact that many of our responses are instinctual. They consist of things that are part of our make up as people, no matter who we are or where we are from. We cannot control many of these traits at all or only partially.

STRESS AND BODY LANGUAGE

When human beings are under stress it is part of the body's response to relieve that stress. Just as if we are hungry, we will feel the need to eat and we get hunger pangs. We can't really control those feelings, they prompt us to take some action. The same is true for stress.

When you have someone in for an interview they are most likely very nervous. This nervousness is the response to the potential jeopardy they feel; they may get in trouble, go to jail, or have to face some other punishment. The body's response to this stress is physical tension of the muscles both large and small.

To relive the stress of this muscular tension we need to move, stretch, or twitch. That is why when we are nervous we pace, verbally snap at friends or family or some people simply perspire excessively.

For the person being interviewed they most likely know that we are watching their every move, so they will try to control their nerves and not pace in the lobby or snap at us. To do these things would indicate they were nervous, and it's a common belief that guilty people act jumpy. Think of your own life experience when you went for your job interview. Were you nervous because you really wanted the position and there was a chance if you screwed up the interview you might not get the job?

Of course you were, so you played it cool, or as cool as you could. You tried to control your response to that stress to convey the appearance you wanted. Same things with people being interviewed for a crime. They will try to LOOK as innocent as possible.

This may take several forms such as:

1. **Stilted behavior;** expecting their rigid posture to control their anxiety.

2. **Slouching** in a chair to show how "relaxed" they are.

3. **Acting "too cool"** for the room as though being there is no big deal.

4. Acting angry, like they are indignant you would suspect them. The anger gives their stress an outlet.

5. Being "in a hurry" to get it over with as though the interview is a waste of their time.

6. Being too cooperative, showing you their desire to help.

7. Tapping their toes or jiggling their legs.

All of these large muscle motor actions are things people can do to control the physical stress they feel. When you see these actions you should take note of them.

An innocent person will feel the same things, but an innocent person will have a tendency to calm down as they engage in conversation and the facts come out. Because they are not mentally hiding anything, their stress is really about the initial contact with you, a representative of the police, not the conversation or interview topic. So you will see those manifestations dissipate over a short time in the innocent person.

A person with something to hide has the stress of knowing what they have done on top of their desire to control their physical movements. When you add to that the energy it takes to tell lies in a conversation, then remember the lies and keep them connected in some kind of logical order, the stress level goes way up.

What you look for here are the small (fine) muscle motor reactions to the stress.

The tiny gestures to relieve the stress that are so small that most people don't even take notice of them, such as:

1. Tapping the fingers.

2. Pulling little bits of lint from their clothing.

3. Wiping their lips or the corners of their lips.

4. Cracking their knuckles.

5. Rocking their head or body.

6. Twitching of the feet.

7. Repeatedly looking at their watch or the clock in the room.

8. Sighing or taking quick deep breaths.

9. Blinking of the eyes.

Over time you will see many different stress relievers, which can include:

1. Scratching a mystery itch on the nose, chin, stomach or other body area.

2. Rubbing the hands together.

3. An unconscious look of fear in their eyes that does not dissipate with time.

4. Being distracted and unable to follow a line of questioning.

5. Rubbing the temples.

6. Moving the lips side to side.

These gestures all indicate a high level of stress of the person who's fidgeting. Innocent people will exhibit the same sort of behavior, but they normally dissipate quickly from the innocent person.

If you see them you should pay close attention. If they don't disappear after a few minutes you should call attention to them and mention that there are signs of nervousness. This comment will add even more pressure to the person who will now be aware of the tics and try to stop both large muscle and fine muscle indicators. This is almost impossible to do.

Creating this internal stress in a person can, over time, break down their will to continue lying. The desire to relieve the stress only can push them to confess.

MICRO GESTURES

The newest area of indicators of stress are called MICRO gestures and appear last. These are the twitching and stress-relieving movements so small that most of them cannot be seen unless you are looking very closely. Many of them are revealed by intently watching a video of the person while being interviewed.

They include:

1. A flinch of the eye.

2. A twitch of a ¼-inch slip of facial muscle.

3. A quick respiration.

4. A body tremor.

These are hard to see and are usually found in people who are very good liars and understand what trained investigators are looking for. They are a whole separate area of study.

OTHER BODY LANGUAGE THINGS TO BE AWARE OF

1. Crossing the arms or legs says—Keep away, I'm locked in here.

2. Constantly pushing back from the table is a safety gesture to provide space from the interviewer.

3. Looking around the room is preparing to mentally escape; they are trying to get away from your questions.

4. Looking side to side can indicate they don't trust you or they are wary of you.

5. Head tilting slightly forward can be a challenge to you, and head down can be a submissive gesture.

6. Clenching the fists can indicate fear or anger.

These and other signs indicate a lot about the person. What's important for you is to look for these things as they are cues to how effective you are being and can guide to advance or back off.

During an interview the investigator and his/her partner should pay close attention to the suspect's body language. How that is interpreted is different for each person, but there are physical signs we can see in how they speak and their body language.

When a person is defeated in sports we see their body language change. We see the same signs in a suspect during an interview when they are defeated in their ability to lie any further.

You might see:

1. The suspect lowers their head.

2. They take deep sighing breaths.

3. They slump their shoulders.

4. They can seem distracted.

5. They wring their hands and make many other gestures.

When you see the suspect starting to display any of these signs you know you are close to either breaking their will to continue lying or they have already reached that point, a good push line and it may all come out.

This is critical – A person realizing they are defeated may either:

1. Surrender and tell the truth, or

2. Realize the consequences of their actions are now imminent and may ask for an attorney, which would end any further conversation.

At this point the use of compassion may be the very thing that keeps them talking and gets the confession out into the open.

You demonstrate that compassion by using a calm tone, reassuring them that you knew they are not a bad person and that realizing what they had done was wrong is an example of that fact. Let them know that you have had other people in the same situation and you have seen that by telling the truth and showing remorse they will have the best chance of getting the least punishment for their crime, because everyone makes mistakes.

Some common beliefs we all share about doing things wrong or illegal are the same for suspects as well as cops.

We all believe, to some extent that:

1. Everyone makes mistakes.

2. Everyone gets out of control sometimes and does and says things that are wrong.

3. Everyone deserves a second chance.

4. Sometime we all do something without thinking of how it will affect others.

5. Sometimes we make bad choices.

6. Sometimes we all act stupidly and do stupid things.

7. We can all be pushed to the point that we can overreact.

These sentiments are part of our culture, you want to use them to your benefit by bringing them up where ever they help you in your interview.

Now that you know what Diminishing and Possibilities are, aren't these things really the same?

Yes, they are. Using one of these and any others I'm sure you can think of can be the one thing the suspect needs to hear from you so they can accept their actions.

Important notes on BODY LANGUAGE

The investigator must look for some specific indicators of Truth and Deception during an interview that are revealed through body language.

When a person is in the police station to be interviewed about a serious incident or crime, they should be very interested in what you, the investigator has to say and ask.

A person that feigns disinterest in the process, looks down, or slouches in their chair like they could care less is indicative of deception. Sitting up, looking directly at the interviewer, almost hanging on your words is indicative of truthfulness.

Other indicators:

Truthful Behavior	Deceptive Behavior
Open, relaxed posture, leans in	Crossed arms, crossed legs
Gets angry when accused	Don't care when accused
Direct answers, listens to full question	Cuts off the interviewer's question
Thinking appropriately before answer	Partial answers, mumbling, no answer
Helps the investigator with ideas	Makes the pool of suspects very large
No flag phrases (I'm religious)	Uses flag phrases (I go to church)
Story makes sense, stays consistent	Story is convoluted and changes

If you see any of these, you must consider the person might be truthful or deceptive depending on what they display in their body language.

Chapter 11 - Case Study: Two Kinds of Guys

An important understanding is how a person evaluates what you say to them. Knowing this can help you choose your words or the things you interject into the conversation. A good example is based on an interaction I had with a man early in my career, before I had any real formal experience interviewing anyone. I call it my "Two Kind of Guys story" and I think it can illuminate the point and the techniques I discovered in this encounter. I have used this technique many times since.

TWO KINDS OF GUYS

When I was a young patrolman, I was assigned to drive a young man to HQ from the field. He had been arrested for the theft of an old woman's purse at a shopping center. The detectives on scene told me I was not to speak to the man but just drive him to the station and have him sit in the interview room of the detective bureau.

The detectives were investigating a series of these purse thefts from older women in the vicinity and it was clear this man was most likely the suspect responsible for all ten strong-arm robberies.

In a couple of the robberies the women, who were in the 70s, were injured when the suspect forcibly took their purses from them. There was no forensic evidence and the victims could not make positive IDs from photos or sketches.

On the ride in I could tell he was nervous. He was in his late 20s and looked like a pretty strong guy. He asked me what was going to happen to him, he even said he found the purse on the ground and was stupid for taking it. This was obviously his attempt to distance himself from the strong-arm robberies and try his story out on the first cop he could tell it to, me.

I told him I couldn't talk to him, but he should just tell the truth when he spoke to the detectives. I knew enough to butter him up a bit and let him know the detectives were good guys, hoping it would help them when they spoke to the guy.

We got to HQ and I sat him down in the interview room and waited for the detectives. While we waited I deflected his crime questions and tried to just talk about sports and family stuff to kill the time. He seemed to calm down.

Eventually the two detectives came in and relieved me. I waited out in the bureau writing my report while they interviewed him.

After about an hour they came out saying the guy was sticking to his story and wouldn't budge; he said he found the purse at the curb and took it. He said he ran when he saw the cop car because he knew the purse wasn't his. The detectives were tired and frustrated and needed a break. One of the detectives asked me to go sit with the suspect in the interview room while they discussed what to do next.

I went back in and sat down. The man seemed OK, but was still nervous. He said he told the detectives the truth but they didn't believe him. He said they were trying to pin a bunch of robberies of old ladies on him that he didn't do. He said he had a grandmother and he would never do something like that to old ladies.

I listened to him and made a decision that could have gotten me in big trouble. I decided to try and talk to him a little more. I figured if the detectives didn't get anywhere with him what would it hurt. He had been Mirandized and had waived so I thought I was on good ground to talk to him.

I didn't know what a possibility was at the time, or what diminishing was, but I thought I might get him to talk to me just based on the way he reacted to me. I was curious and took a chance.

My thought was this: he was scared to admit what he did because it was really a terrible thing to do. I also took note that he mentioned he had a grandmother, and I figured he might feel guilty for targeting these older women as well.

Here's what I said:

"You know, I'm not a detective and I don't know what you talked about with them, but I do know that they believe you did take the lady's purse. The way I see it is this—there's only two kinds of people that would be involved in something like this."

He was not answering me, just listening.

"The way I see it is there is one kind of guy that doesn't care who he hurts. He wants money and he figured a good place to get money is from old ladies that can't fight back."

As I said this, I held my right hand, palm up at about face level. He looked at my hand and I saw a revulsion on his face.

"The other kind of guy is somebody that needed money for something, money for medicine or food for their kids, whatever. This guy would never purposefully hurt anyone especially old ladies. This guy didn't intend to hurt anybody he just needed the money."

As I said this, I held my left hand, palm up just above my stomach creating a real difference between the two hands.

The suspect stared at my hands—first at the higher one then the lower one—he was weighing the choices I gave him.

"What kind of guy are you?" I asked him.

What was interesting with this approach was that I only gave him two guilty choices, if he admitted to either one he was admitting to robbing the victims. The difference was that one of the choices was morally reprehensible, the other was not so much.

I didn't say anything, I just held my hands there. After a second he looked right at my lower left hand and said:

"I'm the kind of guy that didn't mean to hurt anyone."

Inside my head I was jumping up and down. I couldn't believe he confessed to me. But I maintained my composure and said:

"That's what I thought, too."

He nodded and asked me:

"None of them ladies are hurt, are they?"

In reality two of the 10 ladies did get injured, though they were not life-threatening injuries.

"No, none of them were hurt real bad. But you're a big guy, and a couple of the ladies had sore arms when you yanked their purses away."

I then asked him if he would tell the detectives what he told me. He said he would.

I then said,

"You know those ladies had a lot of things in their purses that they would like to get back, like pictures of their families and other personal things. Can you tell me where the purses are?"

He nodded his head yes and said:

"Yeah, they're in the woods next to my house, I'll take you to them."

I thanked him and shook his hand. As I was leaving he said

"Hey officer, will you tell the judge what kind of guy I am?"

I said I would and then I told the detectives what had transpired. I really thought they would be angry, but instead they were thrilled, telling me I did a good job.

Besides the satisfaction of solving the crime and getting the confession, I realized how much I loved talking to suspects and I wanted to do it better. I also realized that the way I talked to him was probably the most important part of that interview.

Even without formal training it was obvious that the suspect felt comfortable talking to me. I also tried to make it seem that he had a genuine reason for taking the purses beside him just being a dirtbag.

I didn't know it, but I was diminishing the description of the crime, and my "two kinds of guys" comment was really a push line.

From then on I read anything I could about the process of interviewing. I talked to detectives and I practiced on everybody I came in contact with. It was clear to me that I could learn to be good at interviews and so can you.

This story points out how we can connect to someone who has very little in common with us on the surface. What we did have in common was family relationships. I used that fact to create the possibilities I threw at him and to which he responded. Maybe it was my newness to the world of crime or the fact that I was younger than the detectives or maybe there approach as more serious than mine that made him uncomfortable, whatever it was he felt, he could connect with me and that was let us have the conversation.

This interaction changed my police career, it can change yours as well.

Chapter 12 - Other Considerations

Now that you have the concepts and techniques backed up by some real-life stories to fill lout the information, we can look at other tings to consider when interviewing people. Remember, we have to look beyond our own life experience if we are to grow in our skills and abilities. The next few topics are food for thought and deserve our consideration.

CULTURAL DIFFERENCES IN INTERVIEWS

Different cultures can have different meanings for words and gestures, or body language. In some cultures it is a sign of respect not to look you in the eye. Don't confuse this with lying or being disrespectful.

My first experiences with this cultural difference can on a call when a man was involved in a domestic dispute and had injured his wife. He answered all my questions and made admissions, but he would only glance at me then look down at the ground. I found this disconcerting and kept telling him to look up at me. He tried but he seemed very nervous to do so. Later I spoke to his parents and asked about their son's refusal to look me in the eye. The father explained that his son was showing me great respect as a police officer. In their culture you do not look in the eyes of authority figures. I remembered this and used it to help me in the future. Understanding the norms of the cultures in your community can help you and help the community.

In some cultures calling a man out on his manhood will put him in a position to tell the truth to prove he is a man.

"A real man would take responsibility for his actions. A cowardly weak man would keep lying."

This understanding came to me from the communities I served. I listened to how people addressed each other during conflicts or street arguments. I listened to how their friends and family members interacted and it became clear that in some cultures the concept of "being a man" trumped all other factors. To be seen as less than a man in terms of accepting responsibility was a greater embarrassment than admitting involvement in a crime.

Knowing this was important, I could use that idea during an interview—"A man would take responsibility and not blame someone else. Are you a man or not?" very often that resulted in an admission, especially if other people were watching and judging the suspects responses.

To others, their families and standing in the community is the most powerful emotion for them. Calling them out as disgracing the family or community can move them to right that wrong by confessing.

Very similar to the example of the real man concept is the concept of bringing disgrace on your family or community. By calling someone out for the damage to their personal or family's standing in the community can be very powerful in moving them to take responsibility.

Playing to people's religious beliefs can be very powerful. Asking them if God would want them to tell the truth can motivate them to confess to stay within the bounds of their religion.

This religious aspect is important. Many people have different faiths, but almost all faiths have a component of confession, or doing right before the eyes of God. To commit a crime might be considered a sin and a sin has to be absolved before the soul can be allowed into the presence of God. No matter how devout the person is, if they have any genuine religious belief you can use this religious component to move them to confess.

By calling them out on their faith you put them in the position of having to live up to their faith requirements or violating those beliefs by continuing to lie to you and not accept responsibility.

In this instance we can say something like this:

"You say you are a woman of faith. Is that right Tina?"

"Yes, I am"

"So, let me ask you this, if God asked you the same questions I am asking you, would you tell Him that you were not at that house when the fire was started?"

Or

"Tina, I see you wear a religious medal around your neck. Are you a true believer in God or is it a more decorative thing?"

"I am a true believer. I go to church all the time"

"OK. Would God want you to lie to me or would He want you to tell me the truth?"

This puts her in the position to deny her faith by lying or tell the truth to be faithful. Really faithful people will choose to be right with God rather than lie.

We also see suspects use religion to try and convince us they are good people who would not commit crime. When they do this they use religion as a shield. You might see a suspect come into HQ for an interview carrying a bible or wearing a really large religious medal. They may invoke the name of God in their defense. They may tell you how they pray every day since the incident seeking Gods help. A person who is not really faithful will use these techniques as an appropriation opportunity ,meaning they invoke religion and wrap themselves in it to give the impression they are very good by virtue of their faith.

Asking few specific questions about their attendance at church and who their pastor is can reveal their true position. Telling them you will follow up with their pastor to get a character endorsement will help a real religious person, a faker will often refuse to give the name of their church or pastor because they know their story will be destroyed- they may tell you

"I don't want to involve my pastor in this situation as a way of putting you off. I would respond that our pastors are the perfect people to get involved when we are falsely accused of a crime. That can usually give you all you need to know.

ADULTS VS. CHILDREN

Dealing with children is more difficult because kids can be very willing to please adults and say what they think the adult wants to hear. They are very easily led or intimidated, which can lead to a false confession or the investigator leading the child to the conclusion the investigator is seeking. Always consult with your DA or Prosecutor's office about interviewing children under the age of 12 or 13. Many agencies have specially trained investigators to talk to kids that age.

Because Juveniles are different than adults you should take a course on interviewing Juveniles specifically, but here are a few things to consider.

- When interviewing people under the age of 18 consider asking open ended questions.

- Kids will look for clues as to what you want from them, don't focus too sharply on a single item, instead give a wider perspective, and ask the child what they now about it.

- Children will often fear telling on their parents or guardians. The parent/guardian is their whole world, good or bad and they may be reluctant to tell you want daddy or mommy or Uncle Bill did.

- Children will protect their friends at all costs. Since children don't have a long-term view or experience in the world, protecting their friends may seem like the most important thing in life. They will lie or change their story to protect a friend.

- Depending on the age of the child the idea of being a "Rat" or a "Snitch" is worse than anything else that could happen to them, including getting in trouble with the law. Sometimes playing one child's story against another child's story can work if the child feels betrayed by their friend.

- Children don't always have a full grasp of timelines when it comes to an event. They may confuse days, dates, or times very easily. Trying to pin them down can be frustrating. Instead of using a timeline as a reference "Where were you at 6 PM, Little Billy?" maybe try using the child's routine as the time line- "Little Billy did you see the masked man before or after you watched Sponge Bob on TV that day?" This is open ended but gives the child a time reference they can understand.

- Children will often remember details days later after you talk to them. Anything could trigger the memory. If you get a call from a parent or teacher saying the child has new information don't jump to the conclusion that they are lying because they didn't reveal the information during the original interview. Instead accept the information openly and ask the child when the remembered the new information. Very often they will tell you what triggered the memory and why they forgot the first time.

- When you are done interviewing a child you might want to ask (And I do this for all interviewees regardless of age) "Is there anything I didn't ask you about this incident that YOU think is important? Very often children will only answer what they are asked about. Then later in the investigation you find out the child had important information they didn't tell you and when you ask, they say "You didn't ask me."

Take your time with children as victims, witnesses, and suspects. They had less life experience they don't always see the bigger picture and their concerns about jeopardy and punishment is different than an adult perspective. Look for my book on interviewing Juveniles coming soon.

Normal vs. Sociopath

Most ordinary people will not be able to lie for a long time, especially when confronted by facts and under stress precipitated by jeopardy and questioned by a skilled interviewer.

It is a normal reaction to the stress of lying to vent and tell the truth, even if it means they will be in trouble. They will feel guilt for hurting others or committing crimes that are socially inappropriate.

The sociopath on the other hand has no problem lying and feels little if any guilt for hurting others; therefore, many of the common tactics we use will have no effect on them. You may have to try other methods such as playing on their sense of self-power or their pride in the actions they took.

Many sociopaths may respond to stroking of their ego about an incident. They don't feel remorse or concern for the victim, but if you comment positively about how the crime was committed, how smart the person who did it must have been or other comment about the person responsible they may take the moment to bask in the glory so to speak and tell you they did it or IF they did it, how they would have done it (famous football player accused of murder did this). This allows the sociopath to connect to the event without taking the normal route of guilt. This is a very complex topic look for my book on investigating crimes committed by sociopaths coming soon.

Older Suspects

Older people tend to respond to respectful concepts and ideas. Doing what's right for its own sake and taking responsibility for one's own actions can be powerful.

Older people have a greater sense of time and right and wrong. Appealing to their life experience and their legacy may move them to be more responsive to questioning that considers their long life and their accomplishments.

Referring to their status as respected elder statesmen in their family or community can also induce feelings of responsibility and legacy for older people.

MENTALLY CHALLENGED PEOPLE

There are so many different mentally challenged people in our society that you must understand exactly what the person has been diagnosed with so that when you are talking to them you know what their capabilities are.

People with mental challenges can overreact based on how you interact with them. Their specific condition can also dictate how they respond and how you should approach them with questions.

Understanding the different types of mental disabilities can help you determine the best way to talk to a person so afflicted.

As a young patrolman I responded to call from a woman whose 17-year-old son was acting up in the home. I had no other information. When I arrived, I found a 6-foot-4-inch-tall 225-pound 17-year-old cowering in the corner of his room. When I talked to him, I realized he had a metal disability that I didn't know anything about. I spoke gently and calmly about respecting his mom. When I told him he could get into trouble if he didn't listen to his mom he reacted quickly and unexpectedly. I turned to talk to his mom, and he jumped on me knocking me t the floor. I never saw it coming. The next ting I know he was choking me and I was seeing little stars in the corner of my vision, I thought I might die. So did his mom. I drew my side arm to shoot him to save myself when his mother hit him with a lamp to stop the assault. It worked; he ran off and hid in another room.

It was only after that event that I learned about his disability and how he reacted to potential "Trouble." I cold have died or killed an innocent young man. Dealing with mentally challenged people is a challenge in itself. You need specialized training. Look for my new book in interviewing the mentally challenged.

I had one other important experience interviewing a mentally disabled young person. A 25-year-old man lived with his 69-year-old grandmother. He was a pleasant young man and articulate enough to understand with only a little effort.

One day this young man got mad at his grandmother and attacked her while she was in bed. He jumped on her and punched her about the head. He poured bleach down her throat and tried to light it on fire. When it didn't light, he ran to his room.

The grandma managed to call for help and I arrived with patrols. We located the young man and took him into custody. At HQ I realized he had a metal challenge, but I wasn't sure what it was. He could speak to me and answer questions and he seemed to understand what he had done.

As we began the interview, I read him his rights which he said he understood, he even asked a few questions about them and then waived them and said he would tell us what happened.

Long story short, my partner and I were not comfortable with his confession. Not because of the facts he presented, he was clear about those. He wanted to buy something for $200 and his grandmother refused to allow him to buy it so he wanted to kill her and use the money in her purse.

We were not comfortable because it didn't seem he really understood the gravity of his actions even though he said he wanted to murder his grandmother.

We called the county prosecutor and made arrangements for a mental evaluation. When the case came to court the judge found that he did understand his Miranda rights and he waived them at the moment they were read to him, but based on the expert testimony of the mental health professionals who testified within a few minutes, due to his condition, he had no understanding of the process. Based on this he was correctly diverted from the criminal justice system into the mental health system for treatment. Grandma got better and the young man got help.

Lesson learned—Mental health challenges are very diverse and require the interviewer to use great care and caution.

FALSE CONFESSIONS

Making Someone Confess (False Confession)

Some people believe you cannot get an innocent person to confess to a crime, which is not true. You can certainly make an innocent person confess for many reasons, including exerting intense pressure on them, overriding their will to resist, the desire to end the questioning, creating so much stress that confessing is seen as the only means of relief.

And exhaustion can also lead to a false confession.

The tools of a skilled and unrelenting interviewer are very powerful and can lead to a false confession. Always make sure you are doing the right thing. As law enforcement officers we are sworn to protect the rights of everyone.

My partner Chuck and I learned first-hand that people will confess to things they did not do for many reasons, such as the ones listed above. Case in point, "I took a peek."

We were investigating a report that a 35-year-old man had physically molested his 15-year-old stepdaughter several times including fondling her breasts and penetrating her vaginally with his finger. Very serious sexual assault charges to be sure.

We took a statement from the victim's mother and then from the victim. There were inconsistencies in the statements that they attributed to the daughter being embarrassed to tell her mom everything; not unrealistic.

Next, we located and interviewed the suspect. He denied all allegations, he professed his innocence and love for his wife and his stepdaughter. We persisted. The statements were strong, the victim had details that included the basic facts.

The family lived in a one-bedroom garden apartment. There was a small "den" near the rear entrance. Mom and stepdad used the bedroom, the victim used the den as her bedroom. The den room was adjacent to the apartment buildings parking lot. When the stepdad came home from his 3 PM – 11 PM shift at a local factory he entered the apartment through the rear door, went through the den bedroom of his stepdaughter and into the main apartment.

It was during these late-night arrivals that the victim said the suspect would molest her in her bed while she was sleeping. Her mom was said to go to bed about 9 PM each day and was not aware of the abuse. It was only recently that the victim told her mother what was happening to her when her stepfather returned home from work.

The victim described the stepfather as pulling back the sheets on her bed and touching her breasts and vagina. She said she woke up during these events but could not stop him. She did not tell her mom because she didn't want to upset her mom and her stepdad's relationship. She finally decided to tell when her mom and stepdad were having relationship problems.

That information set the stage for our interview. We began by asking about the family relationship, the suspect was very honest about the problems he and his wife were having, but he denied touching his stepdaughter sexually.

We continued to pursue his story and take it apart as best as we could. His answers were direct, good eye contact, no history of sexual abuse in his record and he made very strong denials. Chuck and I were not comfortable with this interview. The suspect was not just holding on strong to his denials he was breaking down and still holding onto them. He professed religious beliefs that made these allegations very painful for him, but he would not make any further admissions.

After several ours of this back and forth we tried a tactic of male bonding. We said we were all men in the room and we understood that he and his wife were having relationship problems including a non-existent sex life and based on that we could understand if he did some inappropriate things to his stepdaughter. We were trying to diminish his actions and help him rationalize them. He did not take the bait, but we continued.

After a break and some coffee, we tried again. At about hour number four of the interview we could see signs of defeat, he was weakening. We decided not only to diminish the words we used but to diminish the criminal conduct, we wanted to get him to at least admit to pulling down the sheets on the bed and touching the victim's breasts.

Chuck and I later talked about this and we both had the same feeling that we were overriding the suspects will to resist. He was tired and so were we, and it was showing on all of us. At one point we asked him to at least admit that he did sometimes stop and stare at the young victim laying in the bed, that se was a pretty girl and he found her attractive. We asked him it is was Possible, that he just readjusted her sheets and accidentally touched her breasts. He did admit to that.

This admission gave us hope that we were onto new territory, that maybe he was ready to give up lying. We continued along these diminished lines: he was not related to the victim other than by marriage (Rationalizing), That he didn't hurt her (She was asleep) and he didn't intend her any harm, he was just weak and wanted to "take a peek" at this pretty girl. He was silent for a long minute, he looked at the table and started to cry, then he said—"I did it, I pulled off her sheets and took a peek at her breasts, I did it."

While this was a breakthrough, it didn't feel right. We then proceeded to add in the other allegations, and he admitted to them, but his descriptions of what he did were very different from the victim's descriptions, very different. It also seemed that he was offering admissions for whatever we brought up. Each time we asked him, "what else did you do?" he stumbled around mentally searching as if he could not remember.

After he finished Chuck and I got him a soda and said we wanted to take a statement from him, he agreed and said he should go to jail for what he did. Chuck and I conferred at this point about the huge differences in the suspects descriptions and the victims, they were stark. It was troubling.

We were intending to talk to him further when the phone in the bureau rang, it was the victim's mother. She said she took her daughter for sex assault counseling and the daughter had new information to tell us. About 30 minutes later the victim and her mother and her counselor arrived.

We sat down to discuss the new information before we would go back in to the suspect. The victim then told us that her step-father never touched her sexually, she made up the story because of the problems her mother was having in her relationship with her stepfather. She thought if she said he touched her, he would be made to leave; she didn't realize he would go to jail. The counselor backed up her recantation as genuine.

The victim said her stepfather came in one night in February and the cold wind blew in with him. He closed the door and as he was walking by, he stopped and pulled the covers up over her to keep her warm. She said she thanked him at the time and went back to sleep. She thought of that incident when she created her story.

Again, long story short: The victim's recantation made sense with this new information. We were all convinced that the victim had now told the complete truth, but we had a man admitting to sexual assault.

Chick and I knew we had pushed the suspect too far. We had overridden his will to resist us. He confessed because we made him believe he did the things alleged, at least in his weakened state he believed it. We went back to him and went over his story, which changed again because he was making it up for us. Made up stories often do that. After a very painful hour we told him he was not being charged and that his wife was waiting upstairs to take him home. He was emotionally drained. He then said he told us he did it because he loved his family and we made him believe he did bad things he just couldn't remember doing them. The whole family would later go to counseling together and separately to address the issues in their family.

Chuck and I learned a very important lesson about the power of interview, and mental stress. We knew for sure that false confession are real, and we made sure we never pushed a person like that again if we had concerns about the story or the facts we were investigating. We now knew the signs to look for in a false confession. Pay attention to what's going on in your interview, and follow your gut.

INTERVIEWING SOMEONE AFTER A VIOLENT ARREST

Of course, if the interview comes on the heels of a violent arrest, it will be harder for you and the subject to relate and interact.

If that is the case, here are a couple of thoughts to smooth the situation so you can get a conversation started:

1. If you made the violent arrest out in the street it is usually better to have someone else interview the subject and in fact many departments make that a policy.

2. If you didn't make the violent arrest then you can begin to build a bond with the subject by creating some separation between the arresting officers, yourself and the subject. You can do this by:

    a. Asking the subject if they are alright; do they need medical assistance (for cuts scrapes bruises etc.). This shows your concern for them and masks your allegiance to the other cops.

3. Ask them directly—"What happened out there." You can expect to get their side of the story right or wrong. Whatever they say don't argue with them this is not the time for that. You can further show your impartiality and create more space and credibility with the subject by asking a few clarifying questions. Be careful not to get into too many Internal Affairs type questions because that investigation will be separate from yours; instead try to paraphrase whatever they tell you. If they ask you what you're going to do about it, tell the person you will advise the sergeant exactly what the person told you. THEN tell

the subject very clearly you are sorry that happened to them; no matter what a person did or didn't do, no one should get beat up.

4. Then make it clear that YOU are not one of the cops that arrested them, you are there to get the truth and their side of the story. If you are genuine and sincere you can usually move on from here.

5. Offer them a drink or something to eat.

6. If their clothes are torn or wet, offer them dry clothing or a new shirt. This shows your compassion for them. Keep in mind their clothes could be evidence, this tactic could also serve to get the clothes without a more prolonged argument.

7. Make sure they know they are being videotaped (if that is your policy and the policy of your state). Tell them that is to make sure that the video is done to ensure everyone is treated fairly and their rights are protected.

THE END OF THE BEGINNING

This brings us to the end of the book, and the lessons I wanted to pass on. I covered them in-depth. I tried to provide stories that were real and relevant and would help you understand the context and concepts for becoming a great interviewer.

We all have this ability, but it has to be developed. You can be a great interviewer and a value to your organization with your skill set, but most important you will be a part of the justice system that brings results for victims and our society.

Like the title of this segment states, this is the end of the beginning. Take this information, use it every day, get good at what you do, be curious and ask a lot of questions. Remember, Every interaction with another person in an interview. This reality offers a lot of opportunity to practice and it is practice that will help you develop YOUR schtick, and your "go- to's" when interviewing any one for any reasons. Watch out for salesman/ and saleswomen, now you have the edge in the deal.

Our job is a noble one, a profession of hero's big and small. Solving any crime is a win for the good guys and gals. Protect the victims who need us and put the tragedy we see every day in a place that it can't hurt you and get out there and solve crimes!

Thank you for getting this book and reading it. If I have given you anything new to consider I see it as an honor to be one of the blocks in your career. We are all in this together, be a part of the solution not a part of the problem.

Look for other books in our series, each one offers insight and knowledge learned from years out in the field and was developed through relationships with many great interviewers, all of whom I have had the privilege to know.

Review your notes and consider purchasing the companion video to this course, *The Art of Interview*. Owners of the book get a discount. Visit info@ipvideocorp.com for more information.

But the best thing you can do is practice the techniques on a regular basis and study the concepts so they are clear to use in your everyday schedule.

Being able to conduct a great interview has other benefits for you as well. When you are interviewed for a promotion or transfer or if you seek employment after the job, you will be in a great position to control that interview as well.

Thank you again for joining me on this journey and for buying this book. I hope it helps you every day during your career and life. Keep your eyes open for other books I have planned on police-related topics and school security as well.

Conclusion

The art of interview is like a deep and wide river. When we start learning how to conduct good interviews, we see the surface and learn to ride the rapids and currents; but as time goes on, we learn to navigate what's beneath the waves.

It is here, under the waves, in places we can't always see very clearly, that our experience will help us. As we learn more about human nature, interview more people, participate in more complex cases, we grow to understand and remember more of the process.

People are an amazing life form. We are made up of so many different pieces that make all of us unique. For the investigator, understanding these unique aspects offer an opportunity to use them in our interviews because the person's traits, and therefore their actions at a crime scene or with a victim, can be identified uniquely as well.

We also share many similarities just by being human. People in the range of normal, even criminals, can often respond to the same things as our non-criminal friends. It is in understanding these commonalities in people that can move an interview forward.

Combining the two elements of uniqueness and similarity in your growing understanding of people will help you connect the dots in an interview and give you the advantage. Always practice honing your interview skills. As I've mentioned, every interaction with another person is an interview, learn from every encounter.

Be curious, be dedicated, listen to the voice in your head that offers insight based on your experiences and do your job well. Our society needs you.

— Lt. J Pangaro

Index

Action imperatives.. 17
Active Listening skills.. 4, 18
Adults vs. children.. 118
Bait Possibilities.. 20
Barricaded person... 53
Baseline... 20, 66
Body language.. 102, 108
Build a bond... 78
Burglary 94
Case study; sex offender interview............................. 82
Children, dealing with 118
Classic interview.. 33
Cleansing breath 81
Cognitive dissonance....................................... 7, 9, 11
Communication... 23, 40
Compassion 77
Concepts of Interview and Interrogation..................... 41
Conducting proper investigations 7
Confessions 35, 38, 41
Cooperation... 34, 35
Corrections officer.. 1, 2
Covey, Stephen R... 18
Crime scene.................................... vii, 31, 33, 43
Criminal investigations procedure............................... 2
Cultural differences... 115
Curiosity... 46
Deception; recognizing 55, 91, 108
Denial of involvement 28, 95, 97
Detective; role of 2
Different cultures 115
Diminish.. 69, 72, 95
Diminishing the crime 69
Display compassion 69, 80
Eye contact.. 10, 31, 124
False confession 123
False confessions 35, 41
First goal of an interview.. 75

First impression... 57
First obstacle.. 33, 95
Fortifying breath 81
Four main techniques 69
Gauging responses.. 66
Gifted speakers.. 45
Guilt... 25, 28, 37, 43, 55
Human compassion 26, 27, 29
Human interaction 7, 27, 40
Inner motivations 36
Intentions 53, 69
Interrogation
    transition to... 99
    understanding.. 98
Interrogation techniques... 43
Interview after violent arrest 127
Interview preparation 89
Interview, stages of... 97
Introspection 4
Jeopardy... 7, 12, 22, 27, 28
Lights, camera, action... 64
Manipulate... 53
Mediocre investigator... 36
Mental game 74
Mentally challenged 121
MICRO gestures 105
Miranda Rights.. 55
Miranda warnings 57
Murder, committing 93
Nonverbal communication 40, 101
Normal vs. sociopath 120
Offer alternatives 69, 76, 80
Older suspects... 120
Parsing words 54
Patrol officer; role of 2
Personal inventory 89
Physical evidence.. 42
Plausible Possibility 34
Police custody.. 57
Political correctness.. 94
Possibilities 33, 89

Power of human touch.. 26
Power of Why 49
Pre-Crime conversation....................................... 61, 66
Pre-Interview conversation....................................... 61
Professional greeting.. 31
Promises.. 35
Psychopath 37
Push line... 27, 100
Rationalize the suspect's actions............................... 72
Recordings; video or digital 64
Respect ....viii, 12, 34, 36
Right mindset xvi
Robbery, committing 93
Self-introspection... 4
Selling drugs 93
Servant Leadership x
Sexual assault, committing....................................... 93
Signs of defeat.. 28, 125
Sociopath 37, 38, 120
Stilted behavior 103
Stress 102
       body language 102
Theft 94
Trust.. 34, 40, 42
Truthfulness.. 34, 35, 108
Two kinds of guys 109
Unwitting 4
Violent arrest... 127
Why.. 96
Words mean things 69